In the Beginning

In the Beginning

Beginning

Critical Concepts for the Study of the Bible

James W. Aageson

Concordia College

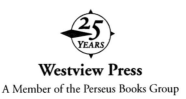

Westview Press

A Member of the Perseus Books Group

Copyright © 2000 by Westview Press, A Member of the Perseus Books Group

Published in 2000 in the United States of America by Westview Press, 5500 Central Avenue, Boulder, Colorado 80301–2877, and in the United Kingdom by Westview Press, 12 Hid's Copse Road, Cumnor Hill, Oxford OX2 9JJ

Find us on the World Wide Web at www.westviewpress.com

Library of Congress Cataloging-in-Publication Data
Aageson, James W., 1947–
    In the beginning : critical concepts for the study of the Bible / James W. Aageson.
        p. cm.
    Includes indexes.
    ISBN 0-8133-6620-8
    1. Bible—Introductions. I. Title.
BS475.2 .A155 2000
220.6'1—dc21
                                                                                    99-087540

The paper used in this publication meets the requirements of the American National Standard for Permanence of Paper for Printed Library Materials Z39.48–1984.

10   9   8   7   6   5   4   3   2   1

For Erin, Anne, and Megan
That they may always be critical readers

Contents

Tables and Figures

Introduction

For Instructors

Having introduced students to the modern critical study of the Bible over many years, I have discovered that it is relatively easy to introduce students to information about the Bible and its interpretation, but it is much more difficult to help students think like biblical interpreters—to raise important questions and to find the means to address them with skill and sophistication. For me, this latter task is the difficult part of teaching courses on the Bible, and it is precisely this task that introductions to the Bible often do not do very well. Standard introductions to biblical content and to interpretive methodology often omit or bury deeply within their scholarly discussions the elementary but important concepts and procedures that enable students to become effective thinkers and readers of the Bible. Most often, in my judgment, students are assisted by having these concepts and procedures brought to their attention quite directly in the beginning of their study.

Consider, for example, the following questions: What happens to a tradition when it moves from oral to written expression? How are hypotheses developed? How are truth claims made and decided? What is implied by the difference between historical and literary approaches to the Bible? How do religious traditions develop and change over time? What material form did and do the biblical texts take? How were texts written and copied? What is implied by the concept of canon? What is the concept of purity, and how did it function in ancient Judaism? What are the differences between archaeological investigation and textual biblical study? How might the Bible fit into a liberal education? These questions receive little attention in standard introductions to the Bible, and yet these are exactly the kinds of questions that prepare students to grapple with the Bible in serious and complex ways. The sixteen short essays that follow are a modest attempt to raise such questions and thus to introduce students to a process of inquiry that will enable them to use more effectively the complex introductions and resources that will be put before them later.

The essays are freestanding and represent different trajectories through the complex world of biblical interpretation. They do not appear in a strict thematic sequence and can certainly be used in any order that seems appropriate to the instructor or students (see the summary of chapters later in this introduction). The essays are not exhaustive treatments of the respective topics, nor are they intended to answer all of the questions they raise. Each essay confronts a topic that I have found to be important and useful in my teaching, and I hope that my approach leads students into a dimension of each topic that might provide a foundation for future study.

More than mere information is at stake here. A process of thinking and learning is involved—a process that I hope will be aided by these brief excursions into the realm of biblical interpretation. If these essays sow even a few seeds of curiosity and critical thinking, then they will have succeeded, for then the fresh sprouts of creativity will begin to grow and will in turn produce their own seeds. This is learning and education at its best.

For Students

These sixteen short essays are written for those of you who are beginning the critical study of the Bible. They are born of my own teaching experience and are designed to help you think creatively about biblical material and the issues that arise from the study of this material. These essays will introduce you to ways of thinking about the Bible, about the interpretation of biblical texts, and about the role of the Bible in religious communities. This book has only one goal: to help you begin a process that will unlock the richness of biblical material and biblical study. In thinking seriously about the Bible, critical minds will be honed. And in bringing passion and curiosity to the study of the Bible, enduring wisdom may even be achieved.

Each of these essays is purposely kept short and written in a style that is accessible to most beginning students of the Bible, whether they be eighteen or eighty. Where the concepts appear to be difficult or the style less than inspiring, I ask your indulgence. But more than that, I ask for your effort and persistence at seeking to understand. Work is the prerequisite for most good things, and this is no exception. In a world where critical thinking and communication skills are needed as never before, these are not idle matters. The ability to grapple with concepts and texts is critical and may mean the difference between being educated or not. As Isocrates said: "Education's root is bitter, its fruit is sweet."

Furthermore, in a world where religion has an enormous capacity for good and evil, the ability to make critical distinctions and humane judgments about religion and things that pass for religion is essential. A good place to begin this process is with texts, traditions, and ideas that lie close to the heart of our culture, civilization, and religious heritage. For Jews and Christians (as well as for Muslims) and for all those who live in Western culture, the Bible is one such text. The traditions and the ideas surrounding the Bible are as old as they are formative. They are of current interest and value, even though they are ancient. Their study gives us a sense of our past as well as our present, and it gives us the opportunity to learn the habits of mind and heart so important for modern life, so important for modern religious life.

Summary of Chapters

Chapter 1:
An Issue of Distance

This chapter is divided into three sections: The Immediate Text, The Remote Text, and The Middle Ground. The chapter deals with the issue of the interpreter's critical distance from the text and raises questions about the way interpreters position themselves mentally and personally before biblical texts, especially when those texts are thought to be directly meaningful to the reader or when they are thought to be distant and without much significance—perhaps even incomprehensible.

Chapter 2:
Two Religions, One Set of Texts

For Jews the Hebrew Bible is the Tanakh and for Christians it is the Old Testament. Essentially the same set of texts have come to be understood in different ways in the two religious traditions. When Christians refer to the Hebrew Bible as the Old Testament, they are in effect imposing a Christian theological designation on the Bible of the Jews. This interpretive and terminological phenomenon is the subject of this chapter.

Chapter 3:
A Matter of Method

This chapter addresses the relationship between biblical material and the methods used to interpret and make sense of that material. Although the chapter does not offer an exhaustive list of interpretive methods, it does offer representative examples of how particular methods (source and redaction criticism) yield new and important insights into the character and meaning of the Bible.

Chapter 4:
From a Hunch to a Hypothesis

The discussion in this chapter turns on the distinction between inductive and deductive thinking in the process of making sense out of biblical material. Hunches and observations about biblical texts give rise to hypotheses from which new insights about texts can be deduced. Both inductive and deductive processes are important in the serious exploration of the Bible.

Chapter 5: What About Language?

A premise of this chapter is that translation is the first line of interpretation. For those who do not know the biblical languages, primarily Hebrew and Greek, the biblical text as it is read is already an interpreted text. Someone, a translator, has made judgments about how the text ought to be translated from the biblical languages into some other language, and that is a process of interpretation.

Chapter 6: To Hear and to See

This chapter deals with the character and function of oral and written tradition. Much of the biblical material did not appear first as written text but as oral tradition. Only later was that oral tradition transformed into the written tradition. In many respects oral and written traditions function differently, and understanding those differences is crucial to making sense of the Bible. Written tradition also implies the care and management of texts, as well as the reproduction of new copies of texts.

Chapter 7: Be It History or Literature?

One of the basic methodological divides in biblical studies is the distinction between historical and literary readings of texts. In reality this is not a hard and fast distinction, but in this chapter these approaches are distinguished for the purpose of illustrating how each asks different questions of biblical texts. In choosing the appropriate approach for the interpretation of a specific biblical text, the determination of the text's genre is also a preliminary and crucial matter.

Chapter 8: The Bible: A Book or a Library?

This chapter addresses the issue of diversity in biblical material. The Bible is closer to a small library of materials than it is to a single book. In terms of genre, as well as in terms of historical and theological circumstances, the texts of the Bible vary from one another. Even within the same biblical book, there is considerable diversity. Recognizing this diversity is an important aspect of being a critical interpreter of biblical material.

Chapter 9:
Like an Ever-flowing Stream

This chapter focuses on the process of development and "recontextualization" of earlier biblical material in later texts. In this ongoing process of development, textual material is used in new contexts that reshape the meaning of the material. Hence, biblical material is used and reused, interpreted and reinterpreted, within the Bible itself. The process of using earlier biblical material in a later biblical text is commonly referred to as "intertextuality."

Chapter 10:
Let's Just Read It Literally

The discussion in this chapter addresses the issue of literal readings of biblical texts and what that might mean for the interpretation of the material. Issues regarding the surface reading of the text, authorial intent, and descriptive accuracy are all discussed as part of the literal interpretation of biblical texts. The conclusion of this discussion is that a literal reading of a text is much more complicated than it appears at first glance.

Chapter 11:
What Is Truth? Fact, Myth
and Moral Critique

For many people, the Bible is closely associated with claims about theological truth. The question that prompts this chapter is, How are truth claims made and determined when thinking about biblical material? Various ways of thinking about truth are considered in this chapter, with the primary goal of claiming that notions of biblical truth should not be reduced to matters of descriptive accuracy.

Chapter 12:
This Canon Has One "N"

The process of producing (writing and editing) the biblical texts is not the same process that brought them to the point of being considered sacred scripture or canon. These are two different processes. The discussion in this chapter reflects on the canonization of both the Hebrew Bible and the New Testament. The results of the canonization of the Hebrew Bible (Old Testament), for example, also vary in different religious traditions: Jewish, Roman Catholic, Greek Orthodox, Russian Orthodox, Protestant.

Chapter 13:
The Three Legs of Interpretation

This chapter deals with the constituency for whom biblical interpretation is generated, the location of the interpreter, and the function for which the interpretation is intended. These three elements related to the "who," "where," and "how" of interpretation affect how people use and understand biblical material.

Chapter 14:
A Question of Purity

As the discussion of this chapter illustrates, the notion of religious purity plays a significant role in early Jewish and early church tradition. Understanding the purity implications of ancient religious life often brings biblical texts into sharper focus than would otherwise be the case. The categories applied by modern anthropologists to questions of purity can also help us make sense of these religious practices and texts.

Chapter 15:
Digging in the Text and in the Dirt

The claim of this chapter is that our understanding of the world of the Bible and of the texts of the Bible is aided both by people who study and interpret texts and by those who uncover and make sense of material remains (textualists and archaeologists). These two tasks involve different forms of interpretation and analysis, but working together both those who interpret texts and those who work with material remains contribute to our comprehension of the Bible.

Chapter 16:
The Bible and the Examined Life

Many students who engage in the study of the Bible do so not for professional reasons or as part of a major program but for the sake of their liberal arts education. This chapter suggests ways the study of the Bible might contribute to the examined life and the education of students, some of whom are overtly religious and others not.

I

An Issue of Distance

The Bible as an ancient set of documents as well as a set of texts that make up the sacred scriptures of Jews and Christians presents the modern reader with some peculiar interpretive challenges. One of the most basic is the reader's personal and conceptual distance from the text. Do readers perceive the words of the Bible to be God's word addressed directly to them? Is the Bible thought to be close to one's own life and the concerns of the day? Or is it remote and foreign? Is the Bible so strange and difficult that it seems impossible to make sense of it? Or do readers find themselves somewhere in the middle on these issues? For many people the Bible is important and meaningful, and yet at many points it remains impenetrable and incomprehensible. These questions raise the issue of where the reader positions himself or herself before the text.

In an abstract sense, that positioning can be plotted, I would argue, somewhere between the extremes of immediate and remote. This plotting will vary from reader to reader, and it may in fact vary for individual readers as they approach different parts of the Bible. But in every case, readers will position themselves before the text, and that position will affect what they find in the text and how they make sense of it. This also means that one's own circumstance as a reader of the Bible is an important consideration in the reading and interpretation of the Bible.

The Immediate Text

If we think first about the extreme of immediacy, we confront a situation where there is very little distance between the reader and the Bible. In the most extreme versions of this position, the reader and the Bible stand nose to nose, so to speak. Not much separates them. In subtle ways, the author of the biblical text is thought to be rather like the reader. The reader's concerns are the same as the author's, and the author, it is assumed, is directly addressing the reader with God's word, which spans the ages with its message of eternal truth. It may be that the reader recognizes that the world of the Bible and of the biblical authors is vastly different from the contemporary world, but still the reader in this position implicitly assumes that on some level of divine truth there is a direct line of communication that can be apprehended with little or no static to distort the message. If readers who occupy the position of extreme immediacy fail to receive and understand the message of God, they may very well attribute this failure to the fallenness of humanity, which has clouded the wills and minds of readers to the word of God. In this case, an inability to understand the biblical text is thought to be the result of a deep-seated human flaw and not a mere problem of textual interpretation—nor a problem with divine revelation itself.

Readers who assume an immediacy between themselves and the biblical text often think that the meaning of scripture, as God's word, is direct and apparent to all with ears to hear and eyes to see. To dig around under the surface of the biblical text only complicates and confuses what is really quite straightforward. For example, if Genesis says that the world was created in six days, with a seventh day of divine rest, it can be assumed without much further ado that the biblical text is dealing with the issue of *how* the world came into being, in much the same way that we moderns are interested in the issue of how the world came to be as it is. This reading of Genesis makes little allowance for the possibility that the writers of Genesis were in fact thinking about the topic of creation in quite different terms. Or, to take another example, readers who occupy the position of immediacy assume that when Matthew and Luke wrote accounts of the miraculous birth of Jesus, they must have been interested in the issues of historical description or biology, much as it seems on the surface of the texts themselves. Such a reading does not entertain the possibility that for Matthew and Luke very different issues might have been at stake.

The devout also read biblical texts with a sense of immediacy in other ways. Thus countless Jews and Christians listen to the words of the Twenty-third Psalm in moments of distress and, washed over by these words, find comfort and strength in the serene tone and vivid images of the psalmist. In the gentle immediacy of these biblical words, the reader hears the word of consolation. A similar immediacy can be found in John 3:16–18, where the love of God for the world is portrayed as direct and immediate: Because God has loved the world so much, everyone who believes in the Son shall not perish but have life eternal. It is easy to hear these words and feel their power. To sense this kind of immediacy yourself, read the words of these two beautiful texts and imagine that they are words spoken directly to you.

PSALM 23

The Lord is my Shepherd, I shall
not want.
He makes me lie down in green
pastures;
he leads me beside still waters;
he restores my soul.
He leads me in right paths
for his name's sake.
Even though I walk through the
darkest valley,
I fear no evil;
for you are with me;
your rod and your staff—
they comfort me.
You prepare a table before me
in the presence of my enemies;
you anoint my head with oil;

my cup overflows.
Surely goodness and mercy
shall follow me
all the days of my life,
and I shall dwell in the house of the Lord
my whole life long.

JOHN 3:16–18

For God so loved the world that he gave his only Son, so that everyone who believes in him may not perish but may have eternal life. Indeed, God did not send the Son into the world to condemn the world, but in order that the world might be saved through him. Those who believe in him are not condemned; but those who do not believe in him are condemned already, because they have not believed in the name of the only Son of God.

The Remote Text

The other extreme presents the opposite difficulty. The biblical texts are remote, strange, and alien. They are from long ago in a far away place. What could they possibly have to do with modern men and women? Readers at this extreme recognize fully that these texts are human documents that were produced by people who lived in a foreign world—a world that was not shaped by modern science and technology. The biblical authors were primitive in their understanding of how the world works. Their languages and their symbolic conceptions of reality were not the same as ours. Our questions were not their questions, and our concerns were not theirs. The gap that divides us from the world of the biblical texts and authors is great. For some people it may even be so great that it cannot be bridged. In this case the biblical text is simply shrouded in a cloud of obscurity, if not outright irrelevance.

In the most extreme versions of this perspective, the Bible is of interest largely as a museum piece to be preserved and studied by a handful of antiquarian experts, at most. For all practical purposes, it is too remote to speak to the concerns and desires of modern people.

Some ancients may have thought that the world was created in six days, but we know better. People in the world of Jesus may have thought that divine power intruded into the ordinary affairs of human beings, resulting in miraculous healings, resurrections, and births; but we moderns know that the world does not work that way. Furthermore, there appear to be morally and theologically questionable things in the Bible. Divine vengeance and wrath are often thought to be an affront to the religious sensibilities of modern people. In biblical imagery, violent language is sometimes used against the enemy in such a way that it seems to make the Bible suspect as a basis for contemporary ethical reflection.

I have purposely presented these extremes as a way of illustrating the issue of distance. These descriptions may not represent the position of any single interpreter of the Bible, but they do illustrate the reason why the position of the reader before the text is vitally important for the matter of textual interpretation. These extremes illustrate as well that reading and making sense of the Bible are a matter of the reader's own self-understanding, as the Bible is approached and encountered as a text to be read. The trajectory of interpretive interest is both forward to the text itself and backward to the circumstance of the interpreter himself or herself. As the circumstance of the interpreter shifts, so is the distance of the interpreter from the text of the Bible apt to shift on a continuum from immediate to remote. Many people have experienced this kind of shift when they have dramatically changed their religious convictions and their view of the Bible. They do not look at the Bible the way they once did, and they do not see themselves in relation to the Bible the same way as before. The two passages quoted below are offered as examples of biblical texts that strike many modern readers as distant and foreign. Read these texts and imagine the distance that separates your world or moral frame of reference from theirs.

EXODUS 7:20–21

Moses and Aaron did just as the Lord commanded. In the sight of Pharaoh and of his officials he lifted up the staff and struck the water in the river, and all the water in the river was turned into blood, and the fish in the river died. The river stank so that the Egyptians could not drink its water, and there was blood throughout the whole land of Egypt.

MATTHEW 10:34–39

Do not think that I have come to bring peace to the earth; I have not come to bring peace, but a sword. For I have come to set a man against his father, and a daughter against her mother, and a daughter-in-law against her mother-in-law; and one's foes will be members of one's own household.

The Middle Ground

If this issue of distance is important, how might we think about it in terms of both the academic study of the Bible and the study of the Bible in communities of faith? Here we ought to think in terms of *critical distance*. Let's look first at the academic approach to the biblical texts.

The academic study of the Bible is based on the critical analysis of the biblical documents. Here argumentation, rather than unsubstantiated assertion, about the meaning of the Bible is the mode of operation. For this argumentation to take place, readers should position themselves at some critical distance from the texts, so that more than one's own reflection can be seen in the Bible. The documents should be removed at least some distance from the reader's own immediate sphere of interest. When one is too close to virtually anything, a sense of perspective and proportion is difficult to achieve.

As has often been said, the best way for people to know about their native culture is to live in another culture. Or if they want to learn about their native language, they should learn another language. The assumption is that if we really wish to learn about those things that are close to us, we ought to gain the distance that learning another possibility can provide. Likewise, in biblical study the exposure to alternative explanations can give one a sense of perspective, indeed critical distance, that enables the reader to see the text in new ways. In this approach to the text, the interpreter's judgment about the text is always open to revision in light of further study and new insights.

Ideally, the academic study of the Bible occupies the middle ground between the extremes of immediacy and remoteness. If this approach to the study of the Bible is to achieve meaningful explanations of biblical texts, there will also be an effort to keep the text from becoming too remote. Any serious attempt at explanation of biblical texts will prevent the Bible from becoming so distant that it is beyond explanation. Every effort will be made by serious students to make their explanation of biblical texts comprehensible to some contemporary audience. By learning more and more about the world of the Bible and methods of cross-cultural analysis, serious students of biblical texts will try to bring the texts close enough to make meaningful statements about them. The pitfall for those who have devoted considerable study to the Bible is to have become so convinced by their own arguments and conclusions that they cease to be open to alternative explanations. A new immediacy to the text has been achieved, but at the expense of sacrificing both a continued openness to and a critical distance from the text.

As the Bible functions in the community of faith, it may not be primarily an item for critical analysis but an instrument for the edification of the faithful through study, preaching, and devotion. Nonetheless, here, too, the study of the Bible should occupy the middle ground and attempt to avoid the extremes of immediacy and remoteness. For increasing numbers of people in our culture, including people within Christian churches, the Bible has become distant. It has receded to the point where it seems incomprehensible and sometimes even irrelevant. In effect, the Bible has ceased to be canonical, the sacred scripture to which one turns for guidance and nourishment.

To be sure, there is little in modern Western culture that naturally assists the process of understanding the biblical text. If anything, cultural influences move in the opposite direction. But this means that religious communities have the doubly urgent task of bringing the Bible into their horizon of understanding and importance. If the

Bible is to continue to serve as a foundational text that exerts a form of constitutional authority, then the extreme remoteness of the biblical texts must be overcome. Imagine that the American Constitution was still considered authoritative but no one any longer knew anything about it or paid any attention to it. For all practical purposes, it would have ceased to function as an authoritative text, despite the lip service that people might give to it. This imaginative situation is in fact a reality with regard to the role of the Bible in many contemporary religious communities. For such communities, the issue of distance, bordering on extreme remoteness, is a problem that cannot be ignored, if the Bible is in fact to function as a canonical document.

Religious communities that wish to take the Bible seriously and responsibly need to overcome the remoteness of the biblical text, but they also need to avoid the trap of immediacy. Even in religious communities, a measure of critical distance remains a crucial part of the interpretive task. When all distance is lost and the reader blithely assumes that the meaning of the Bible, as a word of divine address, is self-evident, the biblical text can lose its capacity to challenge the faithful reader; it can lose its capacity to confront the reader with a prophetic critique that calls the reader to account. In these circumstances, the Bible has, in effect, been made to confirm the reader's view of reality and mode of life. It can no longer disconfirm and challenge the reader, because it has been tamed by the reader's own expectations. When a measure of distance is maintained, the texts of the Bible still have the potential to surprise and unsettle the reader. They can maintain a freshness that keeps them vibrant and alive for the people who hold these texts to be scriptural.

In both academic and religious uses of the Bible, the issue of distance from the biblical texts is a matter worthy of consideration. It is an issue that for better or worse will affect how those documents are engaged, read, and interpreted. Maintaining a critical distance will cause astute readers to think about their own place in the world, as well as their own place before the biblical material that they seek to study and understand. Although the matter of distance is an abstract concept, it is crucial for understanding the dynamics involved in the process of biblical interpretation. Interpretation of the Bible is a complex undertaking, not least of all because it involves a study not only of the world of the biblical texts but also of the reader's own world and conceptual frame of reference. The study of both worlds is critical for a responsible reading of the Bible.

2

Two Religions,
One Set of Texts

Two great religious traditions, Judaism and Christianity, appeal to virtually the same set of Hebrew texts as having divine authority. Yet informed people in these two traditions refer to these common materials using different terms, and that terminological difference is significant for understanding how these religious communities think about the interpretation of these texts. In Christianity these Hebrew texts are identified as the Old Testament, and in Judaism as the Tanakh. For Jews, properly speaking, these texts could not be the Old Testament. Judaism has no New Testament in the strict sense of the term, even though they have later documents that have considerable religious authority. When Christians refer to the first portion of their Bible as Old Testament, a Christian theological designation is being imposed on these documents in light of Christ and those texts that later came to be called the New Testament. In the earliest transformation of these texts into the canonical scripture of Christianity, they were in no sense thought of as the Old Testament. This designation was a later development of the church, and one that presupposed the theology emerging in the early Christian community.

The designation Old Testament, in my judgment, is perfectly good terminology for Christians when referring to these texts, but it is important to understand what this identification implies and that it is not an appropriate designation for the Jewish text. Of course, despite this terminological difference between Jews and Christians, critical approaches to study of the Bible have given people from both religious communities an opportunity to examine their different approaches by appealing to some common historical, literary, and religious understandings that move beyond the narrower concerns of the respective religious traditions. In that process, common ground has often been found between scholars coming out of the two communities, new understandings of these texts have been developed, and presumably a new level of mutual understanding has been achieved. That is clearly to the good for people in both communities. Nonetheless, the differences between the Jewish and Christian designations of the biblical text remain important.

Implications of the Designation *Old Testament*

Frequently, in Christian communities, the designation *Old Testament* has also subtly implied the inferiority of these texts relative to the New Testament. At best, the Old Testament texts contain the prophecies that are fulfilled in Christ, and at worst the Old Testament is simply prolegomena to the culmination of salvation history in the New Testament. In some Christian worship services, the Old Testament lesson is not even read consistently; and in others, if the service is suspected of being a bit too long, the Old Testament reading is omitted to save time. In subtle but unmistakable ways, this treatment of the text suggests that the Old Testament is of less value than the New Testament. It also reinforces the sense that the Old Testament is not really important and can easily be ignored. This depreciation of the Old Testament is, of course, not universal across the Christian tradition, but it is common enough to be suggestive.

Another dimension of this subtle depreciation of the Old Testament among Christians is the lingering legacy of Marcion. Marcion was a second-century Christian who thought that the God of the Old Testament was a God of wrath and judgment, quite unlike the

God of mercy who was the God and Father of Jesus Christ. On these grounds, Marcion argued that the Old Testament ought not to be part of the Christian Bible. To put it bluntly, Marcion still bedevils some corners of Christianity, even though he was deemed to be heretical by the emerging church. Marcionism can still be found among Christians who see in the Old Testament not a God of grace and covenant but of cruelty, retribution, and violence. It is easy enough to see how a reading that selects only such things from the pages of the Old Testament reinforces the inferiority or at least the secondary nature of the text. In this case, the Old Testament is both archaic and theologically suspect. Although such a reading of the text is not uncommon, it is far too simplistic.

Another dimension of this lingering Marcionism among Christians is its overall anti-Judaic twist. If the Old Testament is inferior to the New and if Jews are the people of the Old Testament, it would seem to follow that Judaism is inferior to Christianity. Furthermore, if the God of the Old Testament is a God of wrath and judgment rather than a God of mercy, grace, and forgiveness, it would seem to follow that Jews are in league with a rather unappealing, if not despicable, God. The upshot of this view is that Jews had better get on board with Christianity or they will be left behind on the day of salvation. The sad fact is that the Christian separation of the New Testament from the Old tends for obvious reasons to go hand in hand with anti-Judaism and anti-Semitism.

It is worth remembering that Jesus and his earliest followers were Jews and that the only scriptures they had were the Jewish scriptures. They would not have known what a New Testament was. Furthermore, they certainly did not think of these materials as being inferior or as representing a God of wrath and condemnation. Early church tradition itself speaks against Marcionism and the denigration of the Old Testament. The main branches of early Christianity also rejected the anti-Judaic implication of Marcion's claims, a rejection that critical and morally sensitive readers of the Bible should consider, since it makes clear the dangers inherent in a Marcionite reading of the Old Testament.

The Relationship Between the
Old and New Testaments

Within various Christian traditions, different theological emphases have affected the relationship of the Old and New Testaments to each other. Differing understandings of this relationship have been present from the beginning, as is apparent in the ways that the New Testament books themselves deal with material from the Old Testament. For example, Matthew uses much of his Old Testament material from a prophecy-fulfillment point of view, whereas Luke seems to fit Old Testament material into his view of salvation history. Paul's use of Old Testament material often seems to suggest that what was true in the scriptures, correctly understood, and in Israelite history is also true in the present in light of Christ. The other New Testament authors each have their own distinctive ways of construing the Old Testament.

Among the great theological traditions of Christianity, the Lutheran and Reformed (Presbyterian) theological traditions provide a good example of differing understandings of the relationship between the Old and New Testaments. Lutherans, with their Christ-centered Pauline theological emphases and their views of the law, have often seen the two testaments as implicitly disjunctive, whereas the Reformed tradition, emanating from the Swiss reformer John Calvin, has traditionally taken a more theocentric view of the two testaments, with the result that they are thought to relate more closely. In the New Testament texts, both emphases can be found, and it is not hard to see how both views have come to life out of those earliest documents of Christianity. In any case, such examples make it clear that the meaning and value of the Old Testament is affected by how these texts are understood in relationship to the documents and theologies of the New Testament.

Interpreting the Old Testament

Thinking about the Old Testament as distinct from the Tanakh is more than an issue of semantics. The different designations imply

different ways of reading and interpreting the biblical text. If
Christians read Old Testament texts in light of, or alongside of, the
New Testament texts and bring to bear their convictions about
Christ as the Messiah of Israel, this will undoubtedly affect how a
great many Old Testament texts are understood. Jews will read and
interpret these same texts quite differently. Looking at a portion of
the fourth servant song from Isaiah 52:13–53:12 will illustrate this
point.

ISAIAH 53:2–6

For he grew up before him like a
young plant,
and like a root out of dry
ground;
he had no form or majesty that
we should look at him,
nothing in his appearance that
we should desire him.
He was despised and rejected
by others;
a man of suffering and
acquainted with infirmity;
and as one from whom others
hide their faces
he was despised, and we held
him of no account.
Surely he has borne our infirmities
and carried our diseases;
yet we accounted him stricken,
struck down by God, and
afflicted.
But he was wounded for our
transgressions,
crushed for our iniquities;
upon him was the punishment that
made us whole,

and by his bruises we are
healed.
All we like sheep have gone
astray;
we have all turned to our
own way,
and the Lord has laid on him
the iniquity of us all.

The servant described here may well refer to Israel, a wounded nation upon whose people the iniquity of "us" all was laid. In the historical circumstances of the Babylonian exile, during which time this text was written, the trauma of the people of Israel is clear, and now the prophetic claim that this suffering is for the transgressions of others clearly situates the covenant people of Israel at the center of God's redemptive purposes. Through the punishment of Israel, "we" were made whole. Understood in this way, this is an extraordinary image of Israel's place in the purposes of Yahweh, and in Jewish ears this text has the potential to bring to mind powerful notions of servanthood expressed on behalf of others. Even if this text should be understood to refer to an individual, a servant from within Israel, for Jews it can conjure up images of Israel as a servant people through whom divine purposes are enacted and through whom the nation of Israel is restored.

Whenever people familiar with the Christian tradition read this text, it conjures up images of Christ. This connection is immediate and direct. For some, there is virtually no possibility that these prophetic words could be about anyone other than Christ. The connection with Christ is simply self-evident. This is a classic example of reading the Tanakh as the Old Testament. Although Christians claim that this text from Isaiah refers to Christ on some deeper theological level, there is no sense on the historical level of the text that it could refer to him, since it was written more than 500 years before his birth.

For the writers of the New Testament who alluded to this Isaiah text and echoed its words, the prophetic images became a way of understanding the suffering and significance of Jesus on the cross. What did the horrible death of Jesus mean? What was the significance of the Messiah's death at the hands of the Roman soldiers? The words of Isaiah gave the early church a way of making sense of the redemptive implications of Jesus' death: "He carried our infirmities. . . He was wounded for our transgressions. . . Upon him was the punishment that made us whole." The application of these poignant words to the death of Jesus enabled his early followers to understand his crucifixion as a redemptive death for "us" all. The early church proclaimed that in death Jesus brought God's redemption into the world.

In the beginning, the early followers of Jesus understood Christ to be the fulfillment of divine purposes, and in turn they searched their Jewish scriptures for clues about his arrival as foretold by prophets of old. Once these connections were made, the scriptures could be read as pointing forward to Christ and to his redemption of the world on the cross. In those interpretive procedures, the scriptures of the Jews ceased to be read as the Tanakh and became the Old Testament. Ever since, Christians have read Isaiah 53 and other similar texts in light of their faith in Jesus as the promised Messiah of the Jews.

Critical readers of the Bible do not need to abandon their religious and theological convictions, but they are invited to understand how and why these texts common to Jews and Christians are often read differently. Such an understanding contributes to a developing self-awareness that is crucial if one is to be a critical reader of the biblical material; it is also vital if Jews and Christians are to understand one another and to interact constructively. Furthermore, these texts may come to life in interesting and new ways when Jews and Christians sit around the same table and read them together.

3

A Matter of Method

Most forms of scholarly investigation reckon with a basic distinction between material and method. Simply put, the material is the *what* of investigation and the method is the *how*. In the case of biblical study, the material is, of course, the literature of the Bible, but it is also the historical and social context of the biblical texts. In a different field of investigation—biology, for example—the material is composed of all living things—both plants and animals. In the field of sociology, the focus of investigation is the social character of human life. And in the study of the heavenly bodies and their movements, astronomy, once again one finds the particular focus of investigation. What any investigator wants to learn about and study is the material content of that investigation. This is no less true of literary texts or religious phenomena than it is of the physical or natural world. The objects of investigation are simply different.

In the intellectual world after Darwin and Einstein, however, it has become increasingly evident that the position of the investigator in time and space is not fixed and clearly affects what the observer observes. Although the theory of relativity was, of course, developed by physicists to explain certain features of the universe and physical matter, social versions of the concept of relativity have spilled over into the investigation of human culture as well. Likewise, although theories of evolution developed through observation and study of the biological world, it soon became apparent to nineteenth-and twentieth-century thinkers that social development, if not social evo-

lution, is a fact of human life that affects all investigation of natural
and cultural phenomena. It has become increasingly difficult to argue that there is any fixed point from which human observers can
observe the world with any meaningful sense of detached "objectiv-
ity." Human observers always occupy some vantage within the
world as they seek to investigate its features. The upshot of this aspect of our existence is that what we see when we investigate something is affected by the way we look at it, which in turn is affected
by the vantage from which we look. This is no less true in the study
of biblical texts and their historical contexts than it is in other forms
of human observation.

Interpretive Method

With this fact in mind, we should not be surprised that biblical interpreters have devoted so much attention to the issue of method. We
might say that method, or the *how* of interpretation, is simply a disciplined and self-conscious way of approaching biblical texts. Concern with interpretive method is, at its core, a concern with *how* the
reader of these texts reads them and with what the reader in fact is
looking for. Once again, the reality of interpretation is that what an
interpreter finds in the texts corresponds in some measure to the way
that person looks at them. Although concern for interpretive method
is a highly disciplined and sophisticated area of biblical study, the
underlying implication applies to both the most casual and the most
highly trained reader. It is not finally a matter of whether or not
readers will approach the Bible armed with their own ways of reading the material from a particular vantage point. It is, rather, a matter of which approach the reader employs and of how self-conscious
the reader is about his or her approach. Any astute interpreter of
texts, including biblical texts, will invariably be compelled to think
about these issues; they are not optional for anyone who wishes to
be educated in these matters.

Over time, scholarship has developed its own specialized approaches to the study of the Bible. And these methodological tools
have in turn become the objects of further investigation, as scholars

have analyzed and argued about not only the *what* of the biblical text but also the *how*. It is not my intention to give an exhaustive list and explanation of the methods that have been developed for the study of the Bible. Those can be found in most good introductions to biblical interpretation. My only goal is to illustrate the principles involved in the interplay between material and method, as these work themselves out in the act of biblical interpretation. With this goal in mind, I will focus on two illustrations of *how* scholars interpret the Bible.

Source Criticism

Biblical scholars studying the Pentateuch (the first five books of the Tanakh/Old Testament) and the Gospels (Matthew, Mark, Luke, and John in the New Testament) in the eighteenth and nineteenth centuries came to realize that these biblical books are in all likelihood based on prior sources (either oral or written) that have been incorporated in the final literary text as it now stands in the Bible. If that is true, then it should be possible to unravel these sources, identify their respective theological and religious peculiarities, and then place them in their own specific historical circumstances. This effort came to be known as "source criticism."

What "source criticism" meant for the interpretation of many biblical books was that the final form of the text, as it presently stands in the Bible, need not be the only focus of interest. The reader who is interested in sources looks beneath and behind the surface of the text and in the process begins to see a web, in some cases a vast web, of oral or written material that precedes the final form of the book. Much as an oceanographer who looks only at the ocean's surface fails to see the vastness of the sea's underwater life and activity, so the reader of the Pentateuch or the Gospels who does not reckon with prior sources will fail to see the depth of the text that comes to light when we take into account its formative history.

To be sure, the work of "source critics" may necessarily be hypothetical and conjectural. Often, especially in the case of oral tradition, the evidence is not sufficient to make conclusive claims about the sources that have been incorporated into the biblical texts. Nonetheless, even if the conclusions about sources are highly conjectural, that does not mean these conjectures are without merit. Such hypotheses may in fact revolutionize the way we look at the material, even though in the end the conclusions cannot be sustained. Some of the most important insights into the Bible have happened in precisely this way. The interpretive conclusions have been proved wrong, but the methodological insights were so penetrating that the biblical material could never again be looked at in quite the same way. The astute reader's line of sight had been expanded to see new things; and once these things came into view, they could not be ignored.

Redaction Criticism

As biblical scholars turned their attention to the sources of the Bible, they also came to realize that if many of the biblical books were in fact dependent on prior sources, then the actual process of editing or incorporating the sources into the final form of the text might be important for discerning meaning within the text. This effort came to be known as "redaction criticism." Here the forms or sources of the text are not the only focus; scholars also consider the way these sources have been shaped and molded in the process of editing.

Once again, an analogy may be helpful in explaining the concept. If a movie director in the process of making a movie shoots thousands upon thousands of feet of film, that vast quantity of exposed film is not yet a movie in any real sense. It is simply the footage out of which the movie will be made in the editing room by a crew of editors. Most of the footage will probably never see the light of day. It may in fact be argued that important characteristics of the movie—its meaning, message, and so on—are actually produced in that process of editing. This is where the joints, juxtapositions, and shaping take place. So if one wants to know in the final analysis how this movie is going to come out, one had better keep an eye on the editorial process. Likewise, in the production of biblical texts, the editor and the process of editing had a significant impact on the final form

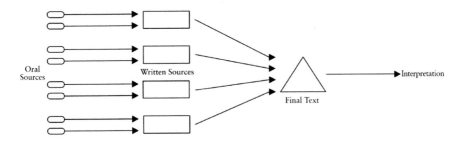

FIGURE 3.1   *The Historical Development of the Text*

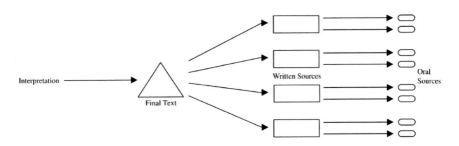

FIGURE 3.2   *The Interpretive Approach to the Text*

of the text; this process is thus the focus of interpretive interest for the redaction critic. Redaction criticism is another way of approaching and reading a biblical text.

At this point a concrete example from the Gospel of Mark will be helpful. Mark 11:12–24 records a story about Jesus, a fig tree, and the temple in Jerusalem. The editorial structure of this account is especially interesting for our purposes because two parts of the fig tree story are used by Mark to bracket the account of Jesus in the temple. We know the structure of this text is not simply random because it is a literary technique that Mark also uses elsewhere in his Gospel. And if we compare Mark's story to the same story in Matthew, we see that the temple cleansing scene is recounted in full and is then followed by the entire fig tree story. Matthew does not split the story of the fig tree into two parts in order to frame the story of Jesus in the temple. But what does this editorial difference tell us about the biblical text? Let's look more closely at Mark's version of the story.

As Mark tells the story, Jesus and his disciples come from Bethany, and along the way Jesus sees in the distance a fig tree. Jesus is hungry, but when he approaches the fig tree he discovers that there are no figs but only leaves, as it is not the season for figs. Apparently angered by this lack of food, Jesus says: "May no one ever eat fruit from you again." Abruptly the scene shifts, and Jesus is in Jerusalem casting the money changers out of the temple. This action arouses opposition to Jesus, and when evening comes he departs from the city. In the morning as he passes by the fig tree, Jesus and his disciples see that it has now withered as a result of the curse. It has dried up. The cursing of the fig tree and the recognition that the cursed tree has withered serve in the text to bracket Jesus' confrontation with the money changers in the temple.

Our comparison of Mark's story with Matthew's (as well as our knowledge that Mark often interrupts one story with another) indicated that Mark's editorial hand is clearly present in this text, but why would he structure his text in this way? What could he be trying to say? The most likely explanation is that Mark uses the fig tree story to interpret the temple story. By framing the story of Jesus' actions in the temple with the story of the cursed and withered fig tree, Mark implies that Jesus has effectively placed the temple under a curse. As the curse of the fig tree results in the tree's withering, so the curse of the temple will result in its demise (which, it is worth noting, is something that did in fact occur when the Romans destroyed the temple either shortly before or shortly after Mark wrote his Gospel). If we are right to read the Gospel in this way, then it seems that Mark did not see Jesus' actions in the temple primarily as an account of its cleansing but rather as an announcement or explanation of its destruction. In this case, the meaning of the text has clearly been shaped by the way the editor structured the story. Without focusing on this editing process, a reader of this text might never be able to see what appears to be at the heart of the story for Mark.

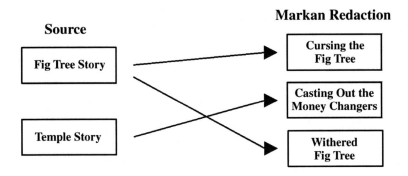

FIGURE 3.3   *Shaping the Tradition*

Source and redaction criticism provide good examples of how interpretive method influences what we see in biblical texts. Many other examples could be used to illustrate how method influences the process of reading this material, but the illustrations I have offered should suffice to make it clear that when the light of a methodological perspective is cast upon the text, certain features of biblical content begin to come into view. The more disciplined that methodological perspective is, the more intense the light is, and hence the more vivid the contours of the biblical texts. These texts are rich and full texts, and advances in methodology have made this only more and more apparent. Issues of "material" and "method" go hand in hand, and they shape the way we think about biblical texts. If you will excuse the pun, reading the Bible is a matter of method.

4

From a Hunch to a Hypothesis

Most readers of the Bible notice things about the biblical text that are unusual or striking, things that jump out from the pages of the text and beg for some kind of explanation. Casual readers may simply bypass these peculiarities and press on to the next page without hesitation. But careful readers and those who wish to study these texts must pause and ponder what these things might mean and how they might be explained. The more serious student will further expand the range of investigation to see if these features of the text exist elsewhere in the Bible or to see if they link up with other features of the text in some meaningful way. What readers find to be unusual in a text may vary from reader to reader, but the fact that there are features embedded within a text that prick the reader's curiosity is important in the formation of interpretive explanations. These curiosity items become the starting points for further study.

Inductive Thinking

To think about this issue in a more systematic way, it is appropriate at the outset to approach a biblical text inductively, that is, to make observations about the text and its character. This is a task of exploration and investigation and of getting as many of these observations about the text out on the table as possible. In many cases, such observation will lead to the identification of a whole series of disparate features of the biblical text. These features may be related to each other in some way or they may not be. The more experienced interpreter will be able to range far and wide in identifying other passages in the biblical text that share all or some of the features of the material at hand. Less experienced interpreters will be proportionately less able to undertake this comparative exercise, of course. But in either case, the procedural principle is the same. Observations are rendered on the particulars of a biblical passage and on its widest possible context.

Throughout this process, hunches and intuition may be valuable in following the various leads of the text. In many cases, however, the hunches will prove to be dead ends. Pursuing a lead that turns out to be a dead end may not, however, be a waste of time. At least one knows where a particular lead does not go, and one may find out later that the insights gained in pursuing the lead link up with some other unexpected observation or feature of biblical material. This inductive exploration of the text is a process that normally requires sustained detective work.

Deductive Thinking and Hypotheses

In sustained and serious interpretive work, the next stage is to devise a way of accounting for the evidence. Can an explanation be offered that will do justice to the available evidence, the features of the text that have been identified? This stage of interpretation is a process that involves constructing a way of making sense out of what has been found. In short, this is work for the mind. It is constructive and creative. It is the work of forming a hypothesis to make sense of the material. The better the hypothesis is able to account for the evidence, the more adequate the hypothesis is. Invariably, hypotheses are able to deal with some parts of the evidence better than other parts; that is in the nature of this kind of work. But a good hypothesis should be able to provide a plausible explanation of the material in a cogent and clear fashion. And even when provocative hypotheses are shown to be inadequate, they may still have the power to generate new questions that in turn can contribute to the formation of new hypotheses. This is a progressive and generative process. It is a process that can open the eyes of the reader to whole new ways of looking at the Bible.

Once the hypothesis that explains the observed evidence in the biblical passage has been elevated to the level of an argument, that argument or thesis can be used in turn as a working assumption to deduce further insights about the biblical text. At this point, the interpreter of the biblical text is working deductively. The interpretive act is not now a matter of simply identifying features of detail or items of curiosity within the text. On the contrary, it is a matter of deducing a cogent explanation of the biblical material from the working assumption that has been set forth to explain the previously identified curiosities. This process can be illustrated best by an example taken from the study of the New Testament Gospels.

The Two-Source Hypothesis

Early in the study of the Gospels it was observed that the Gospel of John is quite different from the Gospels of Matthew, Mark, and Luke. For example, the so-called "I am" sayings in John are not found in the other Gospels, and the emphasis on the "kingdom" in Matthew, Mark, and Luke is minimal in John. The emphasis on "signs" in John is also not paralleled in the other New Testament Gospels. Moreover, the literary style of John is frequently marked by lengthy discourses, unlike the more choppy and clipped style so common in the other three Gospels. And whereas Matthew, Mark, and Luke often recount the same or similar stories from Jesus' ministry, John frequently seems to go his own way in this regard.

For these and many other reasons, Matthew, Mark, and Luke came to be known as the synoptic Gospels. The term "synoptic" literally means "to see together" and suggests that when the texts of the three Gospels are put side by side in parallel columns they exhibit remarkable overlaps. The synoptic character of these three Gospels was evident in the time of the early church, when it was assumed that Matthew was the earliest Gospel, largely because it appears first in the order of the New Testament canon. St. Augustine suggested further that Mark summarized Matthew, assuming not only that Matthew wrote first but also that some type of literary relationship existed between the two Gospels. In spite of this early awareness of the overlaps between the synoptic Gospels, it was only much later that the comparison of these Gospel texts started to elicit persistent questions about the literary relationships between these three accounts of Jesus. Are the Gospel accounts dependent on each other? If so, how is this dependency expressed?

Beginning in the eighteenth century, these and other questions served to direct the attention of scholars, as new and more critical ways of looking at the Gospels began to develop. For example, scholars began to assume that stories and traditions about Jesus tended to be lengthened, and not shortened, over time, as gaps were filled in and unclear places were made clearer. They began to argue that less sophisticated language was generally earlier than more sophisticated language, since it does not make sense that a text that is highly developed linguistically would have been corrupted and made less sophisticated by later transmitters of the tradition. Likewise, these scholars argued that it makes sense to assume that complex concepts and theological motifs are later than simple concepts and motifs.

This approach led to the conclusion that Mark was written before either Matthew or Luke, both of which are longer than Mark, written in smoother and more sophisticated styles of the common Greek language, and display a less primitive manner of presentation. Using evidence internal to Mark's Gospel, scholars fixed the date of its composition close to the time of the destruction of the second temple in Jerusalem in 70 A.D. Most scholars still hold to the view that Mark was written shortly before or just after the destruction of the temple in 70 A.D. In any case, it was written thirty to forty years after Jesus' death, and before either Matthew or Luke.

Over time the careful study of the synoptics tended to confirm the conclusion that Mark was probably written before the other two synoptic Gospels. For example, close observation indicated that almost all of Mark's material about Jesus appears in either Matthew or Luke or in both of them and that there is similarity in the sequence of that material as it is recorded in the various accounts. The conclusion that synoptic scholars drew from this fact was not only that Mark was the earliest of the three but that Matthew and Luke used Mark in the writing of their own Gospels.

Scholars concluded further that Matthew and Luke were dependent on Mark but not on each other when they wrote their respective stories of Jesus. Let me offer a brief example of the kind of thinking that drew scholars to this conclusion. In Matthew chapters 5–7, the gospel writer presents his account of the Sermon on the Mount. It is a highly formal and stylized presentation of Jesus' teaching that contrasts sharply with the presentation that much of the same material receives in the Gospel of Luke. Luke presents the material in a different literary pattern—in different forms and according to a different sequence and different contexts (Luke, for instance, records a Sermon on the Plain—a level place—and not a Sermon on the Mount). Perhaps the two Gospels share this material because Luke is dependent upon Matthew. But does it seem probable that Luke, having read the beautifully formed and constructed Sermon on the Mount, would have disassembled it rather than simply used it as he received it from Matthew? Most scholars think that is unlikely. Luke probably was not dependent on Matthew and got the information in another way. Given the space, I could also offer an account of why scholars think it is equally unlikely that Matthew copied Luke, but the example of the Sermon of the Mount is sufficient to illustrate how scholars approach these texts.

The claim that Matthew and Luke were not dependent on each other was clearly significant and created another mystery, since scholars had noticed in their investigations that Matthew and Luke share some material that is not in Mark. In fact, the wording of this common material, mostly teachings attributed to Jesus, is in some cases almost exactly the same in Matthew and Luke. But if this material is not in Mark, and if Matthew and Luke did not copy each other, then where did Matthew and Luke get this common material? Some scholars answered this question by hypothesizing that Mat-

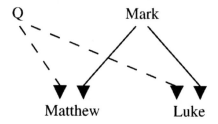

FIGURE 4.1   *The Two-Source Hypothesis*

thew and Luke had a second source. Today, we normally refer to this source as Q, from the German word *Quelle,* generally translated into English as "source." According to this so-called two-source hypothesis, Matthew and Luke drew on two primary sources when they wrote their accounts of Jesus: Mark and Q.

Although Q has never been found by archaeologists and is by definition only that material held in common by Matthew and Luke, most scholars who look at these texts carefully think that Q was a written document. It could possibly have been a stable oral tradition, but in some cases the wording is so close that it is more likely that the writers were drawing on a common written source. Furthermore, the similar sequence of some of the Q teachings as they appear in Matthew and Luke suggests that a written source stands behind Matthew and Luke's use of the material. The existence of the Gospel of Thomas, a noncanonical gospel that was found buried in the sands of Egypt in 1945, also makes it likely Matthew and Luke could well have shared a common written source that recorded some of Jesus' teachings. The Gospel of Thomas makes it evident that such independent sayings traditions associated with Jesus were circulating in the early church.

The two-source hypothesis was developed as a way of making sense of the evidence in the Gospels that points toward a complex literary relationship between Matthew, Mark, and Luke. Although the hypothesis is not subscribed to by all modern New Testament scholars, it has withstood many challenges over the years and is still today the most widely held view. Over time it has been elevated to the level of a thesis, that is, a working assumption from which other interpretive conclusions can be deduced. I can now illustrate this deductive process.

If we locate a story about something Jesus did or said that is recorded in all three of the synoptic Gospels, we might say we have an episode that appears in the triple tradition. As is frequently the case with such stories, the three gospel writers recount the story in different ways. Sometimes the variations are slight, but often they are more substantive. Let us assume that we have found such a story in the triple tradition. It is the same story in all three Gospels, but the accounts differ. These variations in our story of Jesus as recounted by Matthew, Mark, and Luke are worthy of notice, for they may give us insight into the development of the Gospel tradition in general and of these texts in particular.

If we assume the two-source explanation, who then is responsible for these variations among the three versions of the story in our hypothetical example? Beginning with the two-source hypothesis as an assumption about the way the synoptic Gospels developed and relate to one another, we can deduce certain conclusions about these variations and perhaps about some of the theological perspectives of the writers themselves.

The first observation regarding our hypothetical story of Jesus is that it probably has nothing to do with Q. By definition Q is that material common to Matthew and Luke but not, in the main, found in Mark. Since our example is part of the triple tradition, it almost certainly is not from Q. According to the two-source hypothesis, Mark is the earliest of the three Gospels and Matthew and Luke drew material from Mark. Hence, it follows that Matthew and Luke were responsible for the variations. They read Mark's account of the story and modified it in accord with their own perspectives. This conclusion is a simple deduction that follows from the two-source hypothesis.

From the variations in the three versions of the story, we can begin to draw conclusions about why Matthew and Luke told the story the way they did, what their theological perspective was, and perhaps even something about the audience to whom they were writing. If we were to look at the whole of the synoptics in this comparative and deductive way, we could presumably discover all sorts of things about the perspectives of Matthew and Luke. In the absence of the two-source hypothesis, we could not make these same deductions.

The case of the two-source hypothesis illustrates quite clearly the intellectual movement from inductive to deductive reasoning and from a hunch to a hypothesis and eventually to a thesis. The two-source hypothesis serves as a model for the investigation of biblical material and for the development of explanations for curious features of the biblical text. This move from inductive to deductive reasoning is a common conceptual approach used in the study of historical and literary material; in that regard, the Bible is no different. Despite the fact that Jews and Christians consider the Bible sacred, one of the axioms of the modern critical study of the Bible is that it can be studied as any other form of literary or historical material. Hence, methods employed on other texts and types of historical evidence have come to be employed in the study the Bible as well. Not all readers of the Bible subscribe to this axiom, but it has become an assumption of the modern critical study of the Bible. Induction and deduction, hypothesis and thesis are among those tools that are brought to the modern analytical study of the biblical texts.

5

What About Language?

Without learning Hebrew, Aramaic, and Greek—the original languages of the Bible—a person who wishes to read the Bible must rely on a translation. As any one who has studied a modern foreign language knows, translation is the first line of interpretation. It is not normally possible to translate by merely substituting one word for another. Most languages do not have those kinds of simple equivalencies. Moreover, semantic meaning is often fluid and determined by usage in context. Those who translate the Bible must try to understand the vocabulary, syntax, and grammar of the biblical languages so that the meaning and sense of the text can be rendered intelligibly in translation. That is no mean task, but it is necessary if ancient texts are to be made available to modern audiences and not just to specialists in the study of ancient literature.

The complexities of translation are further illustrated by the fact that there are different theories of translation. Some translators argue for a strict rendering of the original, where every effort is made to adhere to the style, syntax, and character of the translated text. Others argue for a much more dynamic understanding of translation, where the sense of the text is sought and where that sense is communicated even when the more superficial characteristics of the text cannot be preserved in the translation. In my own view, the communication of the meaning and sense of the text is more important than the literal rendering. In any event, all translations are not the same, and careful attention to the selection of a translation for serious study of the Bible is important. If one is serious about studying the Bible, then good, reputable translations should always be used rather than paraphrases, loose renderings of the biblical texts. Paraphrases are easy to read, but they often obscure important interpretive elements of the text. They may also make significant interpretive leaps that are not necessarily warranted by the text.

Of course, when a person has the opportunity to study the original languages, that is certainly recommended. Knowledge of Greek and Hebrew gives the student of the Bible one more tool with which to get inside the biblical texts and their world. Study of the biblical languages alerts the reader to the subtleties of biblical thought and to the social patterns that inform the biblical writer's use of the language. Syntax, grammar, and vocabulary are among the building blocks the biblical writers used to construct their texts, and understanding that process of construction can be important in making sense of these texts.

Short of learning the original biblical languages, it is a good idea to use more than one translation of the biblical texts. One can then compare different translations. Such comparison is an effective way of becoming aware of possible translation problems, and it can also alert the reader to alternative ways of rendering the text. Consulting different translations prevents the interpreter from being confined to one translators' words or categories or theory of translation. Let me begin with an example.

Translation and Interpretation:
An Example

MARK 4:11–12

And he said to them, "To you has been given the secret of the kingdom of God, but for those outside, everything comes in parables; *in order that*

'they may indeed look, but not
perceive, and may indeed listen, but not
understand; so that they may not turn again
and be forgiven.'"

   In the Greek text the word translated above as "in order that" is
ἵνα; in this context, the term can be translated in two different ways:
(1) "so that" (result) and (2) "in order that" (purpose). If the Greek
text is translated into English as "so that," then the implication is
that the *result* of the parables is that the people will see and not perceive, hear and not understand. If, however, the text is translated as
"in order that," as it is above, then it appears that the *purpose* of the
parables is to make it so that people see but do not perceive, hear
but do not understand. Obviously, the way the text is translated will
have a dramatic effect on the interpretation of the Markan text.

Translation and the
Problem of Language

Translation of the biblical languages into any given modern language is never finished. It is an ongoing process because current languages themselves are always changing and developing. The English
spoken in various parts of the world today is not the seventeenth-
century English of the King James Version of the Bible. As beautiful
and glorious as the language of the King James Version may be, it is
far removed from the way English is commonly used today. In recent
years, for example, our concern for gender issues and the effect of
language on people has caused many of us to rethink our use of language and the related matters of inclusivity and gender equity. Far
from being removed from these kinds of questions, the Bible as a
canonical text is situated squarely in the midst of these kinds of issues, and the translation of the biblical texts is one component of
that larger set of considerations.

   Not only do languages themselves change over time, but the people who hold the biblical texts to be sacred and authoritative also
come to use different languages. As a result of social and demo-

graphic changes, many Jews and early Christians ceased to speak the
original biblical languages; and, if they were to have direct access to
these sacred texts, the texts needed to be translated into the languages that the people were now in fact using.

Well before the time of Christ, Jews were dispersed to other lands
where they ceased to use Hebrew, and even the Jews who remained
in the land of Israel stopped speaking Hebrew for everyday purposes. Greek increasingly became the common language, particularly in Jewish communities outside Israel. In Alexandria in Egypt,
for example, there was a large and influential Jewish community
that had become highly hellenized. These Jews not only used the
Greek language but also were strongly influenced by the culture of
the Greeks. It is very likely in Alexandria in the third century before
Christ that the process of translating the Hebrew Bible into Greek
began. This translation, known as the Septuagint (LXX), included
some additional books not found in the Hebrew Bible and became a
standard translation for Greek-speaking Jews and early Christians as
they began to move into the Hellenistic world of the eastern
Mediterranean. For most early Christians, the Septuagint would not
even have been understood as a translation of the Bible. It simply
was the Bible. Nonetheless, within the development of both Judaism
and Christianity, the translation of the scriptures into Greek was reflective of the larger social and demographic circumstances of the respective communities as they encountered the world of the Greeks.

For many Jews in the land of Israel neither Hebrew nor Greek was
the primary language. Aramaic, a language related to Hebrew, had
come to be the common language of the people in Israel. Once
again, this created a problem of translation, and the Jews responded
by translating portions of the Hebrew text into Aramaic. The portions they translated were those that were central to Jewish worship.
Over time, these Aramaic translations were standardized and became known as Targums. The Targums give us a glimpse into the use
and interpretation of the scriptures among Jews, perhaps even into
the world of early Judaism and Jesus, though most of the preserved
Targum texts are much later.

Our knowledge of the Hebrew biblical texts and of the Targum material has increased dramatically with the discovery of the Dead Sea Scrolls in the caves of Qumran. Both Hebrew biblical texts and Targum fragments were found there and date from the time of Jesus or before. For biblical scholars, these finds have been of enormous value, for they tell us much about the way textual traditions of the Bible were developing. For students who read the Bible for more general purposes, the discovery of these manuscripts illustrates clearly that these biblical texts and the languages in which they were written are firmly rooted in the social and historical experience of ancient religious communities who used, read, and interpreted the Bible for their own ends.

Translation and the Jesus Tradition

The conventional wisdom is that Jesus' native tongue was Aramaic. How much Hebrew or Greek he may have known is unclear. Being from Nazareth and traveling throughout Galilee, he would certainly have been in the vicinity of Greek-speaking people in Sepphoris and Tiberias. What we do know, however, is that the New Testament Gospels were all written in Greek. If the Gospel of Mark is in fact the earliest of the four Gospels and was written around 70 A.D., thirty or forty years had elapsed between Jesus' death and the writing of the first New Testament Gospel. That means that sometime between Jesus' death and the writing of Mark's Gospel, the traditions of Jesus' teaching and ministry were translated from Aramaic into Greek by his followers. In other words, the New Testament account of Jesus and his ministry is separated from the historical Jesus not only by several decades but also by the translation of Jesus' words from Aramaic into Greek.

It is not clear that the New Testament Gospels are the earliest written documents pertaining to the life of Jesus and his ministry. There may well have been earlier accounts, perhaps in Aramaic, that circulated but were subsequently lost or absorbed into other texts. Hence, it is difficult to say how this translation process took place.

There may have been some translation from written documents, but
there would also have been a natural process of translation that simply took place in the development of the oral tradition. By word of
mouth, the stories about Jesus spread, and, quite naturally, bilingual
people translated them into Greek for people who were primarily
Greek-speakers and no longer knew any, or only a little, Aramaic. In
time, Greek came to be the standard language of the early church because that was increasingly the language of most of the people who
made up the emerging church. Eventually, these new Greek documents, documents that came to be the church's New Testament, increased in authority and came to stand alongside the Septuagint, the
Bible of the early Greek-speaking church.

Translation and the Church

As the church grew and spread farther to the west, it not only arrived in Rome, the center of the Roman imperial world, but eventually came to be enmeshed in Roman life and culture. Not surpris-
ingly, the Roman or Western church began to use Latin, and by the
late fourth century A.D. an effort was made to develop a standard
Latin translation. This translation was produced by St. Jerome and
in the Middle Ages became known as the Vulgate, from the Latin
vulgatus, meaning the "common" or "commonly known." Latin
versions of the Bible remained predominant in the Roman church
until the Second Vatican Council in the 1960s, when the Catholic
mass was opened to vernacular languages. This opening was coupled with renewed interest in the study of the Bible among Roman
Catholics, and in recent decades Roman Catholics have done important work in the area of biblical translation and study.

Significantly, however, what has proved a recent interest for
Catholics has been a focus of Protestants since the sixteenth century,
when Protestant reformers like Martin Luther unleashed an enormous amount of interest in the translation and study of the Bible
with their doctrinal claims that the sole foundation for the church's
authority is scripture and that scripture need not be mediated to the
faithful by priests, by the church. If this claim is true, the scriptures

must be translated into the language of the people—thus Luther translated the Bible into the marketplace German of his day—and there will invariably be a great deal of attention devoted to their study. The reformers believed that the faithful can read and interpret the Bible for themselves, but first they must able to read, and the Bible must be in a language they can understand. Because the biblical texts are or contain the word of God, this understanding is crucial for the church's common liturgical and theological life and for the salvation of the individuals within it. In terms of changing attitudes of authority, education, theology, and church practice the doctrinal claims of the reformers were to have lasting influence on Western culture and on the way people would relate to the Christian church.

In the Eastern churches, the languages were different but the principle was by and large similar. In addition to Greek, the biblical and liturgical languages came to reflect the contexts and circumstances of the churches themselves. From Syriac and Armenian to Coptic and Slavonic, the languages of the people who swore allegiance to Jesus of Nazareth and to the scriptures that testify to him came to be part of the Bible's translation history. In the course of history, the church—Roman Catholic, Orthodox, and Protestant—became a magnificently varied thing, and the versions of the church's Bible have become equally rich and varied.

Biblical Versions

The Bible has been translated into scores of the world's languages and put into the hands of people in every corner of the globe. The student who wants to pursue this topic can consult the articles on versions of the Bible (listed under *Versions* of the Bible) in the *Anchor Dictionary of the Bible*. These surveys cover in some detail the many translations of the Bible in various periods and into various languages.

Translation of the Bible has become big business within the religious community, and large numbers of people have devoted countless hours to the task. For both Christians and Jews, translation continues to be an important aspect of their respective religious work. Translation is important because language is not only instrumental in the formation of texts but also in the very processes of human thought. The difficulties that accompany translation remind us that to read and think about the Bible is to be involved with language, one of the most basic and most important aspects of being human.

6

To Hear and to See

For the unsuspecting reader of the Bible, there is often a tendency to think that the world of Bible is much like our own world. But to think this way is to ignore the distinction between oral and literary culture. The world that produced the biblical documents was largely an oral culture, unlike modern Western culture, which, until the advent of the audio-visual revolution, has been in many ways a literary culture. In the biblical world, people told stories and passed on traditions by word of mouth. Many of these stories were, of course, written down, but those who tended, wrote, and read texts were scribes, a small, professional class of people whose job it was to deal with textual material on behalf of the community. For vast numbers of people who lived in ancient Israel and who lived in the orbit of Jesus' ministry, communication was oral. Large segments of the populace simply could not read or write. Of course, illiteracy in the ancient world did not have the same consequences that it has in most technologically advanced societies, where the vast majority of people are literate and rely to a large extent on written forms of communication. In these cultures, people who can neither read nor write are at a serious disadvantage.

Oral and Literary Culture

In oral forms of communication the ear *and* the eye are the senses that are activated—not simply the eye. More importantly, the different modes of communication function differently and require different ways of organizing information. In oral communication, key words, rhetorical style, euphonic patterns, and patterns of repetition are crucial in creating the mental images that lodge in the mind of the hearer and persuade the hearer of the value and truth of the message. Paul, for example, writing in a dialogical style to the Romans, says: "What then are we to say? Should we continue in sin in order that grace may abound? By no means! How can we who died to sin go on living in it? Do you not know . . . " (Rom 6:1–2). And to the Galatians he writes: "Tell me, you who desire to be subject to the law, will you not listen to the law? For it is written . . . " (Gal 4:21). Through the written words of these texts, one can virtually hear Paul discussing and debating with his opponents in person. The interactive quality of the communication is obvious and suggests that Paul, himself a highly literate man, probably formed much of his material in the give-and-take of oral communication. When this material passed into the written medium, the communication dynamic changed dramatically. Receivers of information now had the opportunity to read information and follow the line of argument with the eye. They could ponder the text's line of thought, as well as hear its rhetorical power.

The early remembrances of Jesus' sayings and deeds were also passed down in the beginning by word of mouth. Jesus did not leave any written records—he may not have been literate himself. For the first years after Jesus' death, there was no overwhelming need to reduce the tradition to writing, not as long as the eyewitnesses to Jesus' ministry were still living, the church was small, and the expectation of the return of Christ was still urgent. Parts of the tradition may well have been written down before the writing of Mark's Gospel around 70 A.D.—Q, for example, may have been written before Mark. Nonetheless, it took some time, perhaps several decades, before the early church crossed a threshold after which the writing of the Jesus tradition came to be more necessary and common. Although the oral patterns did not cease with the writing of the Gospel tradition, the changed medium of expression certainly altered the manner in which the tradition was preserved and communicated.

There came to be an authoritative text alongside an authoritative oral tradition. The oral tradition now had to take into account a literary tradition. Of course, most people remained illiterate, and so the tradition was still presented orally, but the presentation that once depended upon memory, with all the opportunity for variation and amplification that the oral medium made possible, was now based upon a text.

Although not perfect examples, perhaps the easiest way to illustrate the differences between written and oral tradition is to think about the differences between watching television and reading a book, or between writing a letter to a friend and speaking to them over the phone, or between writing an essay and relating an anecdote to a group of friends. The different modes of communication shape the presentation of the material.

The images and the pace of the action on television can affect the emotions as no other medium. But unlike a book, television has difficulty encouraging sustained critical analysis of a subject or issue, and it may not activate a person's creative imagination the way a good written story can. Television is often passive not active. A telephone enables interaction and familiarity between two people in a conversation that only immediate feedback makes possible, whereas a letter facilitates precision in communication and the extended exposition of an idea in a way the telephone does not. A written essay, developing a set of ideas and all of the nuances that go with them, has the capacity to be preserved in the precise form it was written, but a story told to friends is fleeting. It is unlikely that an oral story told among friends will be preserved with any great precision—if preserved at all. For effectiveness, a story depends on the imponderables of vocal tone, facial expression, and physical response. None of these is operative in an essay.

To point out these differences is not to argue for the superiority of one medium of communication over another but to appeal for sophistication in understanding the limits of various modes of expression and the way different modes of expression presume different contexts and affect quite profoundly the way information is organized, presented, and received. These differences are important for understanding the development of the biblical tradition and also for understanding the use of the Bible in different contexts today. Sensitivity to these issues is crucial for understanding the way the Bible and the biblical tradition function in communities of faith.

The Character of Written Texts

When Israelite and early Christian sacred tradition entered into the written medium, a whole host of issues came to the fore that heretofore had not been relevant. How were copies to be made? What sort of writing material should be used? What physical form would the texts take? What happens when different manuscripts of the same text have different readings? Who will have possession of the texts? What about the economic implications of the reproduction and distribution of biblical manuscripts? And who will care for and attend to the texts? All of these questions and many others pertain to the world of written texts in a way that they do not pertain to the world of oral tradition. Furthermore, these issues affect how the texts are used and function in religious communities. To think about the Bible as text means also to think about the material realities associated with texts—in this case sacred texts.

Think first about writing material. Biblical texts did not appear originally in the form of books as we know them now; rather they took the form of scrolls and codices. The scroll obviously affected the way the manuscripts were transmitted. Because no single scroll could contain all of the biblical texts, individual scrolls containing only some of the biblical books circulated independently. These scrolls were bulky and were difficult to transport, particularly compared to modern pocket editions of the Bible so common today. Moreover, the scroll clearly affected the way the manuscripts could be studied and used. For example, it is much more difficult to compare different parts of a scroll text than it is different parts of a text in book form. Ancient manuscripts also appeared in codex form, folded leaves stitched together. The codex was the precursor of the modern paginated book. Both sides of a page could be written on, and more information could be contained in a smaller space than in the scroll form.

The scroll and codex form of ancient texts is not the only way in which they differed from modern ones. Unlike the readily available and inexpensive writing materials of the modern world, the material used to make scrolls and codices was in short supply and, thus, expensive. Parchment, a processed animal skin, was most often used in scrolls; and papyrus, made of matted reeds, was used for both scrolls and codices. These were the common writing materials for biblical manuscripts. Because the material was valuable, it needed to be conserved, and sometimes the same piece of writing material was used twice, with the result that one text was written over another. Manuscripts of this sort have come to be known as a palimpsest (from the Greek for "rub" or "scrape") because before they were used a second time they were scraped and washed.

When additional copies of texts were needed, there was no easy way to produce them. They had to be copied by hand. That was not only time consuming but expensive. If further copies were to be produced, the most expeditious way to do it was for a scribe to read the text aloud while others copied what was read. The practical consequence of this method was that textual variations could enter into the copies that were reproduced. Either the person reading the text or the copyist could make a mistake. On occasion, changes were also intentionally made in manuscripts to correct errors in spelling and grammar, to harmonize corruptions, to clarify difficulties, or to alter the text for doctrinal reasons. Unless otherwise corrected, any copies made in turn from these copies would bear the same variation. Thus, over time, families of texts began to develop that exhibited certain textual characteristics. In fact, as the various biblical manuscripts were passed down, a complex textual tradition developed, with many variant readings for both Old and New Testament texts.

For people in more modern times who have sought to develop critical editions of the Bible, variant readings are a problem. When the manuscript tradition records two different versions of a particular passage of the Bible, how is the most appropriate version to be determined? In response to this problem an entire field of investigation known as "text criticism" has developed. If one looks in a modern edition of the Hebrew Bible or the Greek New Testament, at the bottom of the page one will see an apparatus—a device devoted to identifying all of the known textual variations in the preserved manuscript traditions. A person who knows how to use the apparatus can see all of the variant readings for a passage, as well as an identification of the manuscripts in which they appear. In modern critical editions of the biblical text, the apparatus stands as a testimony to a complex history of transmission and reproduction of biblical material. In some English translations of the Bible, there are abbreviated textual notes that point to this same rich textual history.

With the advent of movable type in the fifteenth century and modern book binding techniques in the medieval world and beyond, the reproduction of texts entered a new era. Manuscripts could be produced more accurately and efficiently. With advances in printing technology over the centuries, texts could be reproduced much more rapidly, with much greater accuracy, at much less cost. These advances, coupled with increased literacy in many parts of the world, meant that more and more people had the capacity to read the texts for themselves. They no longer needed to rely on professionals, whether scribes or clerics, to present the texts to them. By the twentieth century, letter-perfect copies of the Bible were available in vast quantities and affordable to almost anyone who wanted one.

Technology over the centuries has continued to revolutionize the material forms in which the biblical texts come to us. Today, the Bible can be encountered through an audio cassette, or in some cases even an audio-visual cassette. And more poignantly still, computer technology has revolutionized the way biblical texts are presented and used. All of the information contained in the Bible can be stored in computer format as a series of electronic impulses on a microchip, and it takes up hardly any space at all. Furthermore, a few simple commands can reproduce the text of the Bible perfectly. Now one can search through and compare the biblical texts with great speed and ease. Who knows what kinds of technological innovations are still in the future and how they will affect the use and transmission of biblical manuscripts.

GENESIS בְּרֵאשִׁית

[§ₐ] 1 ‏1 בְּרֵאשִׁית בָּרָא אֱלֹהִים אֵת הַשָּׁמַיִם וְאֵת הָאָרֶץ׃ 2 וְהָאָרֶץ
הָיְתָה תֹהוּ וָבֹהוּ וְחֹשֶׁךְ עַל־פְּנֵי תְהוֹם וְרוּחַ אֱלֹהִים מְרַחֶפֶת עַל־פְּנֵי
הַמָּיִם׃ 3 וַיֹּאמֶר אֱלֹהִים יְהִי אוֹר וַיְהִי־אוֹר׃ 4 וַיַּרְא אֱלֹהִים אֶת־
הָאוֹר כִּי־טוֹב וַיַּבְדֵּל אֱלֹהִים בֵּין הָאוֹר וּבֵין הַחֹשֶׁךְ׃ 5 וַיִּקְרָא
אֱלֹהִים לָאוֹר יוֹם וְלַחֹשֶׁךְ קָרָא לָיְלָה וַיְהִי־עֶרֶב וַיְהִי־בֹקֶר יוֹם
אֶחָד׃ פ 6 וַיֹּאמֶר אֱלֹהִים יְהִי רָקִיעַ בְּתוֹךְ הַמָּיִם וִיהִי מַבְדִּיל
בֵּין מַיִם לָמָיִם׃ 7 וַיַּעַשׂ אֱלֹהִים אֶת־הָרָקִיעַ וַיַּבְדֵּל בֵּין הַמַּיִם אֲשֶׁר
מִתַּחַת לָרָקִיעַ וּבֵין הַמַּיִם אֲשֶׁר מֵעַל לָרָקִיעַ וַיְהִי־כֵן׃ 8 וַיִּקְרָא
אֱלֹהִים לָרָקִיעַ שָׁמָיִם וַיְהִי־עֶרֶב וַיְהִי־בֹקֶר יוֹם שֵׁנִי׃ פ
9 וַיֹּאמֶר אֱלֹהִים יִקָּווּ הַמַּיִם מִתַּחַת הַשָּׁמַיִם אֶל־מָקוֹם אֶחָד וְתֵרָאֶה
הַיַּבָּשָׁה וַיְהִי־כֵן׃ 10 וַיִּקְרָא אֱלֹהִים לַיַּבָּשָׁה אֶרֶץ וּלְמִקְוֵה הַמַּיִם
קָרָא יַמִּים וַיַּרְא אֱלֹהִים כִּי־טוֹב׃ 11 וַיֹּאמֶר אֱלֹהִים תַּדְשֵׁא הָאָרֶץ
דֶּשֶׁא עֵשֶׂב מַזְרִיעַ זֶרַע עֵץ פְּרִי עֹשֶׂה פְּרִי לְמִינוֹ אֲשֶׁר זַרְעוֹ־בוֹ
עַל־הָאָרֶץ וַיְהִי־כֵן׃ 12 וַתּוֹצֵא הָאָרֶץ דֶּשֶׁא עֵשֶׂב מַזְרִיעַ זֶרַע לְמִינֵהוּ
וְעֵץ עֹשֶׂה פְּרִי אֲשֶׁר זַרְעוֹ־בוֹ לְמִינֵהוּ וַיַּרְא אֱלֹהִים כִּי־טוֹב׃ 13 וַיְהִי־
עֶרֶב וַיְהִי־בֹקֶר יוֹם שְׁלִישִׁי׃ פ 14 וַיֹּאמֶר אֱלֹהִים יְהִי מְאֹרֹת
בִּרְקִיעַ הַשָּׁמַיִם לְהַבְדִּיל בֵּין הַיּוֹם וּבֵין הַלָּיְלָה וְהָיוּ לְאֹתֹת וּלְמוֹעֲדִים
וּלְיָמִים וְשָׁנִים׃ 15 וְהָיוּ לִמְאוֹרֹת בִּרְקִיעַ הַשָּׁמַיִם לְהָאִיר עַל־הָאָרֶץ
וַיְהִי־כֵן׃ 16 וַיַּעַשׂ אֱלֹהִים אֶת־שְׁנֵי הַמְּאֹרֹת הַגְּדֹלִים אֶת־הַמָּאוֹר

Cp 1 ᵃMm 1. ²Mm 2. ³Mm 3. ⁴Mm 3139. ⁵Mp sub loco. ⁶Mm 4. ⁷Jer 4,23, cf Mp sub loco. ⁸Hi
38,19. ⁹2 Ch 24,20. ¹⁰Mm 5. ¹¹Mm 6. ¹²Mm 3105. ¹³לשׂכד Hi 28,3. ¹⁴Mm 200. ¹⁵Mm 7. ¹⁶Mm
1431. ¹⁷Mm 2773. ¹⁸Mm 3700. ¹⁹Mm 736. ²⁰לִיַּבָּשָׁה חד Ps 66,6. ²¹Mm 722. ²²Mm 2645. ²³Qoh 6,3.

Cp 1,1 ᵃ Orig Βρησιθ vel Βαρησηθ (-σεθ), Samar bᵃrāšit ‖ 6 ᵃ huc tr 7ᵃ⁻ᵃ cf 𝔊 et 9.11.15.20.
24.30 ‖ 7 ᵃ⁻ᵃ cf 6ᵃ; ins וירא אלהים כי־טוב cf 4.10.12.18.21.31 et 8 (𝔊) ‖ 9 ᵃ 𝔊 συναγω-
γήν = מִקְוֵה cf מָקוֹם ‖ 10 ᵇ 𝔊 + καὶ συνήχθη τὸ ὕδωρ τὸ ὑποκάτω τοῦ οὐρανοῦ εἰς τὰς
συναγωγὰς αὐτῶν καὶ ὤφθη ἡ ξηρά = וַיִּקָּווּ הַמַּיִם מִתַּחַת הַשָּׁמַיִם אֶל־מִקְוֵיהֶם וַתֵּרָא הַיַּבָּשָׁה
‖ 11 ᵃ⁻ᵃ 𝔊𝔙 cj c דֶּשֶׁא cj c עֵשֶׂב 12 ‖ ᵇ l c pc Mss ωℭ𝔊𝔖𝔗𝔙 וְעֵץ cf 12 ‖ ᶜ prb dl cf 12.

FIGURE 6.1 *A Page of the Hebrew Bible with Apparatus. Reprinted by permission of the American Bible Society.*

ΚΑΤΑ ΜΑΘΘΑΙΟΝ

The Genealogy of Jesus Christ

(Lk 3.23–38)

1 Βίβλος γενέσεως Ἰησοῦ Χριστοῦ υἱοῦ Δαυὶδ υἱοῦ
Ἀβραάμ.
2 Ἀβραὰμ ἐγέννησεν τὸν Ἰσαάκ, Ἰσαὰκ δὲ ἐγέννησεν
τὸν Ἰακώβ, Ἰακὼβ δὲ ἐγέννησεν τὸν Ἰούδαν καὶ τοὺς
ἀδελφοὺς αὐτοῦ, 3 Ἰούδας δὲ ἐγέννησεν τὸν Φάρες καὶ
τὸν Ζάρα ἐκ τῆς Θαμάρ, Φάρες δὲ ἐγέννησεν τὸν Ἑσρώμ,
Ἑσρὼμ δὲ ἐγέννησεν τὸν Ἀράμ, 4 Ἀρὰμ δὲ ἐγέννησεν
τὸν Ἀμιναδάβ, Ἀμιναδὰβ δὲ ἐγέννησεν τὸν Ναασσών,
Ναασσὼν δὲ ἐγέννησεν τὸν Σαλμών, 5 Σαλμὼν δὲ ἐγέννησεν τὸν Βόες ἐκ τῆς Ῥαχάβ, Βόες δὲ ἐγέννησεν τὸν
Ἰωβὴδ ἐκ τῆς Ῥούθ, Ἰωβὴδ δὲ ἐγέννησεν τὸν Ἰεσσαί,
6 Ἰεσσαὶ δὲ ἐγέννησεν τὸν Δαυὶδ τὸν βασιλέα.
Δαυὶδ δὲ ἐγέννησεν τὸν Σολομῶνα ἐκ τῆς τοῦ Οὐρίου,
7 Σολομὼν δὲ ἐγέννησεν τὸν Ῥοβοάμ, Ῥοβοὰμ δὲ ἐγέννησεν τὸν Ἀβιά, Ἀβιὰ δὲ ἐγέννησεν τὸν Ἀσάφ, 8 Ἀσὰφ[1]
δὲ ἐγέννησεν τὸν Ἰωσαφάτ, Ἰωσαφὰτ δὲ ἐγέννησεν τὸν
Ἰωράμ, Ἰωρὰμ δὲ ἐγέννησεν τὸν Ὀζίαν, 9 Ὀζίας δὲ
ἐγέννησεν τὸν Ἰωαθάμ, Ἰωαθὰμ δὲ ἐγέννησεν τὸν Ἀχάζ,
Ἀχὰζ δὲ ἐγέννησεν τὸν Ἑζεκίαν, 10 Ἑζεκίας δὲ ἐγέννησεν τὸν Μανασσῆ, Μανασσῆς δὲ ἐγέννησεν τὸν Ἀμώς,
Ἀμὼς[2] δὲ ἐγέννησεν τὸν Ἰωσίαν, 11 Ἰωσίας δὲ ἐγέννη-

---

[1] 7–8 {B} Ἀσάφ, Ἀσάφ p[1vid] ℵ B C (D[Luke]) f[1] f[13] 700 1071 l[185m pt] it[aur, c, d Luke, g1, k, q] syr[hmg] cop[sa, bo] arm eth geo (Epiphanius) // Ἀσά, Ἀσά K L W Δ Π 28 33 565 892 1009 1010 1079 1195 1216 1230 1241 1242 1365 1546 (2148 Ἀσσά) *Byz Lect*[m] l[185m pt] it[a, f, ff1] vg syr[c, s, p, h, pal] Epiphanius Augustine

[2] 10 {B} Ἀμώς, Ἀμώς ℵ B C (D[Luke]) Δ Θ Π* f[1] 33 1071 1079 1546 l[1627m] it[c, d Luke, ff1, g1, k, q] cop[sa, bo, fay] arm eth Athanasius Epiphanius // Ἀμών, Ἀμών K L W Π[2] f[13] 28 565 (700 892 1195 Ἀμμών, Ἀμμών) 1009 1010 1216

---

1 **Βίβλος γενέσεως** Gn 5.1 **υἱοῦ Δαυίδ** 1 Chr 17.11 **υἱοῦ Ἀβραάμ** Gn 22.18 **2** Gn 21.3, 12; 25.26; 29.35; 1 Chr 1.34 **3** Gn 38.29–30; 1 Chr 2.4, 5, 9; Ru 4.12, 18–19 **4–5** Ru 4.13, 17–22; 1 Chr 2.10–12 **6** **Ἰεσσαί...βασιλέα** Ru 4.17, 22; 1 Chr 2.13–15 **Δαυίδ...Οὐρίου** 2 Sm 12.24 **7–10** 1 Chr 3.10–14 **11** **Ἰωσίας...αὐτοῦ** 1 Chr 3.15–16; 1 Esd 1.32 LXX

FIGURE 6.2 A Page of the Greek New Testament with Apparatus. Reprinted by permission of the American Bible Society.

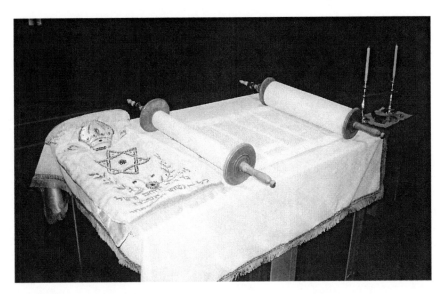

FIGURE 6.3   A Contemporary Synagogue Torah Scroll

FIGURE 6.4   An Old Bound Edition of the Bible

tage vnd die nacht. Vnnd so der morgen ward
gemacht. Der brennent wind huß auff die hew/
schrecken. Sye stigen auff vber alles das lande
egipt. vnnd saffen vnzallich in allen den enden
der egiptier. Das ir als vil vor der zeyt mit wa/
ren gewesen.noch darnach seyn künfftig. Sy be/
deckten alles das antlytz der erd.vnd verwüste
alle ding. Darumb das kraut der erd ward ver
wüst.vnd was der öpffel was an den paumē. Sy
der hagel het gelassen.Vnd nichtz nit vber all
ist belyben grunend an den höltzern.vnd an dē
kreutern der erd in allem egipt. Vmb dye sach

pharaon der eylt vnd rüfft moyses vnnd aaron
vnd sprach zu in. Ich hab gesündet wider ewern
herren got. vnd wider euch . Aber nun vergebt
mir auch die sünd zu der stund vnnd Bitt ewern
herrē got das er abneme disen tod von mir. Vn̄
moyses der gieng auß võ dem angesiht phara
ons.vnnd bett zu dem herren.Der macht ween
eynen starcken wind von dem vndergangk . der
begrayff die hewschrecken.vnd warff sy in das
rott meer.vnd belib keiner in allen enden egipti
Vnnd der herr erhertet das hertz pharaons.
er ließ nit sy sun israhel.Aber der herre sprach

zu moysen.Streck deyn hand zu dem hymel.vn̄
vinster werden vber alles das lannd egipt . als
dick das sy mügen werden Begriffen. Vn̄ moy/
ses strackt die hand zu dem hymel.vnd vorch /
sam vinsternuß wurden gemacht in allem dem
land egipt.Dreyer tag keyner sah seynen bru/
der.noch ward bewegt võ der stat an der er wz
Aber allenthalben do dye sün israhel woneten
so was es liecht.Vnd pharaon der rüfft moy/
ses vnd aaron.Vnd sprach zu in. Geet opfert
ewern herren got.Ewere schaff vn̄ die schwai/
gen süllen allein Bleyben . ewer kind geen auch
mit euch.Moyses sprach. Vnnd du gibe vnnß
die gantzen opfer.vnd sy opffer die wir opffern
vnnserm herren got. vnnd alle sy geen mit vnß
Eyn klos beleybe nit von sen dingen dye vnnß
seyn notturfftig zu dem dienst vnnsers herren
gotz. voran so wir nit wissen was man soll op/
feren biß das wir kumē zu der selbē stat . Aber

der herr hett verhertet das hertz pharaons.
vnnd er wolt sye nit lassen. Vnd pharao sprach
zu moysen.Scheyd dich von mir vnnd hüt das
du fürbas icht sehst meyn antlyt.An welchem
tag du mir erscheynst.so mustu sterben . Moy/
ses antwurt.es gescheh als du hast geredt.Für
bas sih ich nicht deyn antlitz.

Das .XI. Capitel wie

got heß sterben alle die erstgepornen in egi/
pten.vnd wie israhels kinder entlehenten dye
kleynat von den egiptiern.

Vnd der herr sprach
zu moyses.ich rüre noch pharaon von
egipt mit eyner plag vnnd nach disen
dingen läst er euch.vnd zwingt euch auß zu zie/
hen.Darumb so sprich zu allem dem volck das

FIGURE 6.5 *An Illuminated German Biblical Manuscript Showing the Slaughter of the Innocents*

FIGURE 6.6 A CD of the Biblical Text

Technological advances in the handling of biblical texts is not the only factor that changed the role and use of biblical texts in Western Christendom, however. The Protestant Reformation, with its emphasis on the right of every person to read the Bible for himself or herself without the benefit of mediation by the hierarchy of the church, provided an intellectual reason for putting the Bible in the hands of lay people and seeing that they could read it in their own language. Thus it was technology, theology, and ecclesiology working in consort over the centuries that reshaped the way the Bible has been transmitted and used in large segments of the church.

The changes that have accompanied the transmission and the use of the biblical text should remind us that the Bible is not simply a fixed entity, forever unchanging. Think for a moment simply about the material form of the text and the way this form influences how we conceive of the Bible. When most people in the modern world think of the Bible, they think of a book. That is the image that flashes through the mind. But as we have seen, for the ancients that was not necessarily the case. Likewise, it may not be the case in the future either, if technology continues to revolutionize the way the texts of the Bible are presented to us. Consider the change in perception if, instead of reading from the Bible as a book in the context of a festival mass, the lector simply walks to a computer monitor in front of the church and proceeds to call up the appointed lesson for the day. If this ever happens, worshipers will begin to perceive the Bible in a radically different way. The Bible is a form of communication that is always perceived in relation to some material form, and as that form changes, so, too, does our overall perception of the biblical text.

7

Be It History or Literature?

It is self-evident that once the traditions of Israel and the early church were written down and canonized—that is, determined to be scripture—they entered into the realm of literature. To deal with the Bible is to deal with literary material. On the face of it, this is clear, and most beginning students of the Bible would agree, but often there is an accompanying assumption that the Bible is also historical. For many people this assumption means not only that the biblical literature has a historical context, which is obvious, but also that it is, as a "truthful" text, historically accurate. What happened in fact took place as described. To be sure, this assumption raises issues of the "truthfulness" of the biblical text, but it also points to another basic interpretive distinction, namely, the difference between seeing the biblical text as a work of literature and seeing it as a historical work.

In some cases, interpreters simply decide how they will approach biblical texts, whether as literary works or as works about historical reality. This decision may sometimes be more than an interpretive decision; it may be governed by the nature and character of the particular text itself. Some texts in the Bible appear to be descriptive and historical, whereas others appear to be literary productions with little or no interest in describing historical events, as we would normally think of them. Other texts are ambiguous, and interpreters may approach them from both perspectives. Thus the distinction between literature and history may not be an either or matter in the context of interpretation. Conceptually, however, to think about the literary world within a biblical text is quite distinct from thinking about the historical world outside of the biblical text—a world thought to be described by the text. Thus the distinction between history and literature ought to be drawn clearly.

Historical Interpretation

Let us think first about history and historical interpretation. To use a technical term, a historical text is extra-referential, that is, it refers to something outside of and beyond itself. To put it simply, the reading of a biblical text by someone who is interested in history most probably will not focus on the text itself but on some historical reality behind the text, whether that be the historical Jesus, the historical Paul, the history of Israel, or some other aspect of historical biblical reality. The biblical text as history is somehow related to historical evidence. From this perspective, the text is not of interest because of its literary character but because it presents evidence of a historical reality that is of interest to the historian.

To imagine the biblical text as a window is helpful in illustrating this idea. When a person looks at a window, the focus of attention is not the pane of glass but that which is on the other side of the glass. The window provides the access and the means to what is beyond, which is the real focus of attention for the historically oriented reader. Imagine the Gospel of Mark as the pane of glass that gives access to the historical Jesus. For the reader of Mark's Gospel interested primarily in the historical Jesus, the Markan text, as a literary work, is of no more interest than is a pane of glass to someone who looks through a window. The Markan text points beyond itself; it is the means by which historical information about Jesus is transmitted. It provides an evidential link with the object of historical concern, in this case Jesus.

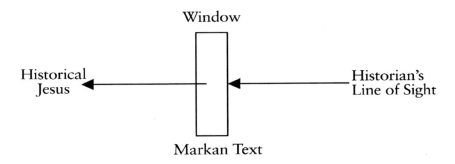

The historian is concerned with what
appears on the other side of the window.

FIGURE 7.1   The Historical Approach to the Biblical Text

The problem with reducing the biblical text to a window is that
even among the most historically oriented books of the Bible the
purpose of these texts is not simply to preserve historical evidence
for its own sake. These texts are national or religious documents
that have some kind of purpose other than to transmit historical evidence for the sake of later historians. Whatever historical material
they may in fact contain is thoroughly shaped by the perspective
from which the material was written. Consider the case of the New
Testament Gospels. The historical information about Jesus contained in these Gospels is contained in documents that have a theological, apologetic, and missionary purpose—they were not written
merely as biographies of Jesus in the modern sense. These accounts
of Jesus are not "objective" reports of what Jesus did and said. They
were written by people who believed that Jesus was the messiah and
that his sayings and actions had some messianic import. In this
sense, they present biased and skewed information about Jesus—at
least from the modern historian's point of view. And yet, almost all
of the substantive material about who Jesus was and what Jesus did
comes from these Christian sources. Thus the people who read these
texts for information about the world of the historical Jesus must

find some means to compensate for the skewed and biased historical information the Gospels present.

We can see the problem by using the metaphor of the window once again. It is as if a person were looking through an imperfect pane of glass or through glass that has been frosted. The light is refracted, and the images are distorted. Most forms of ancient historical evidence may distort the facts, but in the case of the Gospels and Jesus—and for that matter many other parts of the Bible as well—the potential for distortion is particularly prevalent. Some people think that to speak about the Gospels in this fashion is to undermine their veracity and credibility. But this critical historical work, which is the sort of work upon which modern biblical scholarship is founded, need not undermine the value of the biblical material, although it will undoubtedly change the way we come to view and understand the Bible.

To deal with the problem of distortion, New Testament scholars have developed a variety of approaches. Scholars often disagree about which approach should be employed, but for our purposes it will be enough simply to describe some of the possibilities. Certain scholars have approached the Gospel texts and the issue of the historical Jesus comparatively, that is, they have compared a person, a social model, or a different historical circumstance, either in another culture or in ancient Judaism itself, with the Jesus presented in the New Testament. Using this comparative process, which amounts to a kind of historical triangulation, scholars in search of the historical Jesus have attempted to highlight the bias of the New Testament texts and to describe what sort of person Jesus must have been.

Implicit in many of these comparative approaches is the assumption that for a portrait of the historical Jesus to be adequate it must be intelligible relative to other items in Jesus' Jewish context. To put it another way, the Jesus of history makes sense only when he is seen in relation to the Jewish world of his day. Those features of the New Testament accounts of Jesus that are consistent with the world in which Jesus lived have proportionately more claim to being historical than do those features that are inconsistent. To be sure, there are scholarly debates about which Jewish context Jesus should be com-

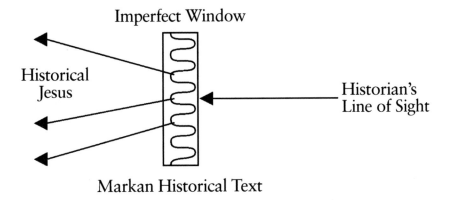

FIGURE 7.2 *The Distorting Effects of the Biblical Text on Historical Evidence*

pared to, but the methodological point is that if Jesus is to be understood as a historical figure, then he must be seen in comparison with some of the features of first-century Judaism.

Other scholars have taken the opposite approach. Using what is variously known as the criterion of difference or dissimilarity, they have suggested that those things in the story of Jesus that are not comparable with anything else have the highest claim to being historical. His early followers would have had no reason to invent stories about Jesus that portray him as idiosyncratic and incomprehensible relative to the world in which he and they lived. Thus those elements in the story of Jesus that make him appear peculiar have a higher probability for authenticity than do those that portray him as similar to others in his world. It is not hard to see that this approach would yield a very different picture of Jesus than an approach that focuses on the similarity between Jesus and his context. If applied rigorously, the first approach would produce a picture of a man who was similar to other figures of his time, whereas the second approach would produce a picture of a peculiar and idiosyncratic man.

These examples illustrate the kinds of questions and concerns that drive historical approaches to biblical texts, in this case Gospel texts. Of course, other parts of the Bible can be approached historically as well.

Literary Interpretation

Historical approaches to the biblical texts are extra-referential; in the main, they are concerned with the world behind or beyond the text. Literary approaches to biblical texts, on the other hand, are internally referential. They are concerned with the internal character of the biblical text as a literary text. Strictly speaking, they are not focused on matters that are outside of the text but on the character and function of the Bible as literature, whether in the form of narrative, poetry, proverb, epistle, or something else.

A literary approach to the Gospels, for example, might read them as narratives, stories of Jesus, with little or no concern for the historical question: Who was the historical Jesus? Instead, the operative questions are of the literary sort: Who are the characters in these stories? How has the author developed them? What are the major events in the story, and how do they contribute to the plot? From this perspective, Jesus is first and foremost a character in a story—not a historical figure. The events that are recorded about Jesus are part of a plot—not mere descriptions of what Jesus actually did or said. And the act of reading the story is an act of entering into a narrative world—not simply a matter of being presented with assembled information about an ancient historical figure.

Of course, if one were to approach a biblical text that had a form other than narrative (a poem, for example), different literary questions would come to the fore. In the next chapter, I will consider some of these questions when I take up the issue of the different types of literature that make up the Bible. For now it is important to see only that even when different literary questions arise, they are literary and not historical questions.

In both historical and literary approaches to biblical texts, the act of reading is of crucial importance. For the historian, the act of reading is an act of discovering and assessing the veracity of historical information. Modern historiography is in large measure a matter of analyzing texts in this way. Of course, students of literature also read texts; but as literary theorists argue, reading is not a passive act. Such scholars argue that a literary work is not simply what is written

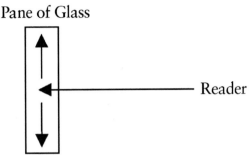

Pane of Glass

Reader

Markan Literary Text

The student of literature is
concerned with the glass itself.

FIGURE 7.3 *Literary Approaches to the Biblical Text*

on a piece of paper; rather it is what is produced when a reader encounters what an author has written. In this sense, reading is a creative and constructive act. Until someone reads a text, it is technically unfinished. It is still only a work in progress. Drawing inferences from the information that is contained in the written text, the reader fills in the gaps. In the process, the reader produces a work of creative imagination.

For literary theorists who focus on the act of reading, a text functions like a mirror. The reader does not seek to look beyond or behind the text but looks into the text and finds that images from the foreground, including the one who peers into the mirror, have become part of the reflected image. This understanding of what it means to be a reader shifts the focus from the world within the text to the world in front of the text, to that encounter between the written text and the reader, where something new is created in the act of reading. Seeing this creative aspect of reading is another important dimension of the study of literature, one that distinguishes modern literary study from most traditional forms of historical investigation, even though the distinction between the two modes of reading is itself sometimes blurred by those searching for new insights into biblical material.

8

The Bible:
A Book or a Library?

Once the biblical texts were canonized and bound together in book form, the tendency to view the Bible as a single book became remarkably pronounced. To be sure, even the most elementary students of the Bible realize that the Bible is made up of many different installments, themselves called books, and that not all of these are similar to each other. But the desire to see them all as part of the sacred story of God and God's people has often tended to obscure the great differences between and among the various books. Despite the theological and thematic connections that draw the canon of scripture into some kind of whole, the literary distinctions between the various books, and even within the same book, should not be ignored or obscured. In this sense, the Bible is not just a book, but a library of books representing many different literary types or genres.

The Diversity of
Literary Genres

If I were to put a poem, a newspaper, an automobile repair manual, and a personal letter in front of reasonably astute junior or senior high school students, they would instinctively know that each of these types of literature cannot be read in the same way. A mental shift must be made as a person moves from one type of material to the next. The standards and parameters of interpretation appropriate for one of the documents will not be the same for the others. The literary genre of the journalist will not be the same as the genre of the poet. The genre of the technical manual writer will not be the same as the person who writes a personal letter to a friend. Each type of writing is fundamentally different, and each needs to be read accordingly.

The book of Jonah is an interesting case in point. If an interpreter were to conclude that the book of Jonah was intended as some type of descriptive historical account, certain considerations would invariably come to the fore. For Jonah to be an accurate historical text, someone by the name of Jonah would have in fact had to have lived, have sought to run away on a ship, have been thrown overboard only to be swallowed by a large fish, and eventually, under protest, have gone to Nineveh, where he preached a message of repentance. If the book of Jonah were in fact a descriptive genre of literature, historical questions would quite appropriately be addressed to it. Likewise the "truth" value of the text would be determined in relation to its genre and character as a descriptive text.

But if Jonah was never intended to be a descriptive historical piece of work but rather a narrative designed to communicate a theological message about some aspect of Israelite religious life, then the mode of reading Jonah would need to shift dramatically. The descriptive accuracy of the events recounted in the text would be of little importance. Instead the reader would be obliged to discern the theological message of the narrative, and the dynamic of the plot would be of considerable importance in understanding the meaning of the text. The "truth" value of the text would not be found in its historical accuracy but in its theological insight and power. It would make little or no difference whether Jonah was actually swallowed by a sea creature. It would make little or no difference whether he was a historical figure who in fact went to Nineveh and preached a message of repentance. The important thing would be to understand the symbolic and thematic development of the plot, as the message is formed through the construction of the story.

Why doesn't Jonah want to go to Nineveh as instructed by God? Why does he run away? Why does he pout when the Ninevites repent? Shouldn't he be happy that they have responded to his preaching? These are important questions when reading Jonah as a theological narrative. Perhaps Jonah does not wish to go to Nineveh because Ninevites are religious outsiders and they have no right to receive the word of God. Perhaps Jonah is unhappy when the Ninevites repent because they repent en masse. Such success a preacher has rarely had, but Jonah is angry because outsiders are not to respond this way. They have simply added insult to injury. To put it crudely, they do not live down to Jonah's expectations.

From a theological point of view, the book of Jonah is about religious exclusivism and moving beyond religious boundaries. The story is not, then, about Jonah's miraculous survival in the belly of a big fish for three days. Different things are at stake, and the question of meaning cannot be determined on the basis of historical accuracy. I offer the example of Jonah as an illustration that one's decision about genre will govern the way interpretation proceeds. The more sophisticated and accurate the assessment of the text's genre, the more adequate, presumably, the subsequent interpretation of the text's meaning.

If the determination of genre is important for understanding the Bible, how does the reader figure out the literary type of any given biblical text? The most direct and immediate way is to make a determination based on the internal character of the text. Close analysis of a text discloses much about the genre of the material. Based upon observations of the text, the investigator can draw certain general conclusions about the text's literary type; with the increase of literary skill, these conclusions can become more specific. This process often shows biblical texts to be made up of complex genres and subgenres. Hence, any decision about a biblical book and its genre must always be open to further revision and correction. Books of the Bible may not be of a single piece, and they may require different literary approaches at different points in the text. Attentiveness to the literary characteristics of a biblical text is a necessary ingredient in the process of determining genre.

TABLE 8.1   Literary Forms in the New Testament

The Pauline Tradition	The Gospels and Acts	Other New Testament Writings
The Pauline Letter	Gospel	The Sermon
Forms of Argumentation	Aphorism	Topoi and Admonitions
The Diatribe	Parable	General Letters
Midrash	Pronouncement Story	Apocalypse
Chiasm	Apocalyptic Language	
Apocalyptic Language	and Forms	
and Forms	Forms of Argumentation	
Paraenesis/Topoi	Miracle Story	
Vice and Virtue Lists	Commissioning Story	
The Household Code	Stories About Jesus	
Liturgical Fragments:	Midrash	
Blessings and	Hymn	
Doxologies	Speech (Acts)	
Poetry and Hymn	Johannine Discourse	
Creeds	Chiasm	
	Genealogy	

SOURCE: John L. Bailey and Lyle VanderBroek, *Literary Forms in the New Testament: A Handbook* (Louisville: Westminster/John Knox, 1992), pp. 7–8.

Determination of literary type can also be aided by comparison with other texts or literary types. Are there literary parallels from the period or other periods that shed light on the text? If there are, these can assist the reader in making literary judgments about the biblical text in question. By comparing other texts or textual types, the character of the material can often be brought into sharper focus than would otherwise be the case. When parallel examples are available, they ought to be used as a means to refine one's sense of textual type in order to achieve greater clarity. Over time, one's literary knowledge and instinct increases, so that the biblical texts can be approached with ever more sophistication. For serious students of the Bible, this is a goal worth striving for.

Serious interpreters of the Bible ought to begin by determining the genre of a biblical text based upon the character of the text itself and upon any comparative models that may be available. However, there are times when readers of biblical texts, for the sake of interpretive experimentation, may wish to assume a particular literary genre when approaching the biblical text. Here a sense of genre is brought to the text, and the interpretive implications of the text are worked out through a reading of the material in light of that genre. For these interpretive exercises to be productive, there ought to be some literary warrant for bringing the selected genre to the text. If there is no justification for bringing the chosen genre to the material, the conclusions will be quite silly. But as an investigative mode, this can be an interesting interpretive procedure, if the experimental genre has some applicability to the material under consideration.

To use the Gospel of Mark as an example, some interpreters have brought narrative understandings of literature to the reading of the second Gospel. This literary type, as opposed to more traditional readings of the Gospel that focus on biography, has lead to many new insights about the Gospel and its meaning. A narrative is not the same literary type as a biography, and the assumption that Mark is a narrative and not a biography leads the reader to different conclusions about the character of the material and its meaning. A narrative displays characters and character development, plot and plot development, setting, point of view, and so on. Most forms of biography have different concerns and express those concerns by means of different literary and structural features. Even if the narrative form cannot, in the end, be sustained as the appropriate genre for the Gospel of Mark, narrative readings of the Gospel have resulted in many important insights into the text. Indeed, they have altered the way that many people now read the Gospel of Mark.

The Diversity of Historical and Theological Circumstances

The Bible is diverse not only because of the many different literary genres and subgenres found within its pages, but also because of the extraordinary variety found in the historical circumstances that gave rise to the biblical texts. Biblical texts emerged out of social, religious, and historical circumstances; and presumably these circumstances left their own imprint on the texts. Hence, there is often a quite direct correlation between the text and the world out of which the text appeared. This correlation is especially evident in the Hebrew Bible, which was produced over the better part of a thousand years. During this period, very different circumstances came to prevail at different times and in different quarters of Israelite and Jewish religious life. These differences are now recorded, if at times faintly, in the diversity of the biblical texts as we now encounter them. Although the New Testament texts were written over a much shorter span of time (somewhat less than a hundred years), they also exhibit considerable variety in their historical and religious circumstances.

Diversity entered into the biblical material not only from the various historical and religious worlds in which the authors lived, but also, in many cases, through a process of textual development over time. Many of the biblical texts underwent elaborate processes of writing, rewriting, and editing that, over time, multiplied the historical circumstances that came to bear on the literary material. The Pentateuchal texts, for example, were written and rewritten over many generations, and the concerns of the later editors came to be reflected in the material. Hence, the Babylonian priestly writers, in their supplementation of the Pentateuchal material, brought a decidedly priestly framework to bear on the Pentateuch as we now know it. Biblical tradition is clearly not a fixed entity but is shaped and reshaped over time; the examples of this in the Bible are multiple.

Comprehensive approaches to the interpretation of biblical texts will often combine both literary and historical judgments that take into account the tremendous diversity of the Bible. In this sense, the Bible is no mere book but a whole library of materials that by the accident of format have come to be presented in book form. Recognizing and dealing with this diversity critically and creatively is crucial, if one is to develop a full sense of the Bible and its meaning.

9

Like an
Ever-flowing Stream

Rarely are religious traditions set in concrete, fixed and unchanging expressions of theological truth. Quite the opposite. Traditions, including biblical traditions, are consistently reshaped, formulated anew, and developed. Like a river that ebbs and flows with the seasons of the year, carving new river bed channels, and sometimes even charting whole new river courses, the streams of biblical tradition move through time, from one generation to the next, one group and historical context to the next, one idea and conviction to the next. Sometimes traditions recede from view only to reappear in some new form, and sometimes they disappear altogether. At other times, sharp turns in one direction or another are made, and radically new traditions and ideas appear on the scene. The evolution of tradition is a complex and dynamic process with many twists, turns, and subtleties. Observing and seeking to understand the nature of these changing traditions has occupied the attention of biblical scholars over many years and is critical for all who seek to understand the Bible.

Form Criticism

Biblical scholars have not been satisfied with the knowledge that biblical tradition develops; rather, they have sought ways of investigating the development of tradition, both its structural and formal characteristics, as well as conscious efforts to reshape it. In the early part of the twentieth century, scholars, focusing on the character of folk traditions, began to identify the relationship between the formal features of tradition on the one hand and its "situations in life" on the other. These scholars argued that by identifying the formal structural features of a tradition, one could discern something about the circumstance out of which the tradition developed and how it functioned in that circumstance. In the jargon of biblical scholarship, this scholarly effort came to be known as "form criticism."

Among other things, "form criticism" has reminded us that although literary traditions and forms are preserved in the text as we have received it, their exact nature may reflect contexts and circumstances that are very different from those that existed at the beginning of the tradition. In other words, the circumstances that spawned the tradition in the first place may be all but lost from view in the new biblical setting that now cradles the material. Even though the text of the material may be essentially the same, the context that supplies the framework for the tradition has shifted. To use the jargon of biblical scholarship, the tradition has been "recontextualized."

An example from the opening of Psalm 118 illustrates the point. In Psalm 118:1–4 the psalmist writes:

> O give thanks to the Lord for he is good;
> his steadfast love endures forever!
> Let Israel say,
> 'His steadfast love endures forever.'
> Let the house of Aaron say,
> 'His steadfast love endures forever.'
> Let those who fear the Lord say,
> 'His steadfast love endures forever.'

These words now appear as part of the Jewish and Christian scriptures, with all of the connotations that the biblical Psalms generate for the faithful. If a person looks more closely at these words, however, certain formal features of the text become clearer. For example, there is a three-fold pattern of exhortation: "Let Israel say," "Let the house of Aaron say," "Let those who fear the Lord say." After each of these instructions, the appropriate response is recited: "His steadfast love endures forever." The Psalm has a responsive or antiphonal quality, as different groups are addressed and invited to respond in identical fashion. Someone, presumably a leader, exhorts the others to respond, and each group in its turn gives the desired reply. The formal character of this text suggests that it was originally part of a liturgy.

If Psalm 118 was in fact part of a liturgy, a further conclusion can be drawn. Liturgies are used in the context of worship, and it appears that some type of worship setting is precisely the situation out of which Psalm 118 emerged. That is its "situation in life." In this case, "form" (liturgy) and "situation in life" (worship) both come into view. In other contexts, the same words might be understood differently and serve a different function. For example, instead of being part of a liturgy prompting the nation of Israel to give thanks for deliverance in battle, these same words might be a private call to those experiencing personal difficulties, inviting them to take refuge in the steadfast love of God where they will be protected from all danger. Or these words might suggest the steadfast love that God has for all people of the world and not merely for Israel and its king. Hence, the developing of biblical tradition shifts not only through direct changes in the tradition itself but through a complex process of "recontextualization."

Redaction Criticism, Recontextualization, and Intertextuality

In addition to form criticism, "redaction criticism," observing the process of how materials are shaped in the process of editing, has also contributed to our understanding of how traditions develop and change. In many parts of the Bible, one encounters evidence that editors have reshaped and recontextualized traditional material. In these cases, new and altered applications of older materials are quite often injected into the developing tradition. These new applications may be subtle or they may be dramatic, but in some sense the meaning and function of the material is altered by the editorial process.

Once again an example will illustrate how editorial context shifts the meaning and function of a tradition. Paul in Philippians 2:5–11 writes:

> Let the same mind be in you that was in Christ Jesus,
> who, though he was in the form
> of God,
> did not regard equality
> with God
> as something to be exploited,
> but emptied himself,
> taking the form of a slave,
> being born in human likeness.
> And being found in human form,
> he humbled himself
> and became obedient to the
> point of death—
> even death on a cross.
> Therefore, God also highly
> exalted him
> and gave him the name
> that is above every name,
> so that at the name of Jesus
> every knee should bend
> in heaven and on earth and
> under the earth,
> and every tongue should confess
> that Jesus is Lord,
> to the glory of God the Father.

Most scholars think that Philippians 2:6–11 is a very early Christian hymn focusing on the figure of Christ. And that view seems to make considerable sense. The text has a virtual metrical pattern, and the imagery of the text clearly outlines the life and fate of Christ as projected by the early church. But notice the context in which it appears in Philippians. If one reads chapter 2:1–5, it becomes clear that Paul is not interested in merely rehearsing the pattern of Christ's life. Paul is addressing a contentious situation in Philippi and seeking to bring harmony out of discord. The Christ hymn is used in a hortatory context—you Philippians should be of the same mind as Christ Jesus, who, as you know, humbled himself and took on the form of a slave. He did not exploit his relationship with God but emptied himself. Now do likewise. By placing this hymn in a new context, a hortatory context, Paul has shifted the function of the material. In short, Paul says, "Imitate Christ." Follow his example. Be rid of the strife and contention that sets one over and against another. If scholars are right about the early origins of Philippians 2:6–11, then Paul has used an old text in a new context, giving the material a quite new and different meaning.

Another, similar way of thinking about development and change in scriptural tradition is to observe the character of "intertextuality" in the Bible, the use of material from one text by the writer of another, later text. The intertextual use of material is a prominent feature of certain Old Testament writings and illustrates the way older traditions were taken up, revised, rewritten, alluded to, or simply reflected in later material. But perhaps the most dramatic example of "intertextuality" is the use of the Old Testament in the New Testament. Paul alone quotes Old Testament material directly about a hundred times, in addition to countless allusions to and echoes of various Old Testament images, ideas, and language. Other New Testament authors also refer extensively to Old Testament material and reflect their own brands of "intertextuality." These New Testament writers turned to the Old Testament not only as a source of authority but also as a source of stimulation, religious nourishment, and prophetic announcement. The Old Testament scriptures provided a powerful symbolic and literary world that resounded through the minds and writings of the New Testament authors. But the authors always adapted and recontextualized these intertextual images so that they fit new arguments, new literary requirements, and the new world of first-century Christianity.

The History of Traditions and
the Formation of the Canon

Another variation on this theme of development in biblical tradition is often referred to in scholarly circles as the "history of traditions." In this case, scholars identify a particular tradition and plot its development in different texts, religious communities, historical contexts, and literary forms to see how the tradition has evolved. In some cases, but not often, it may even be possible to trace lines of dependence from one text to another. Mostly, though, we simply see how the tradition has changed and been applied in new circumstances. For example, a given story recorded in the Old Testament can be traced through its development in the Old Testament material, as well as its development in the New Testament and in all of the material outside of the Bible, such as the Dead Sea Scrolls, the literature of the later Rabbis, and other Jewish material of the period not found in the Bible.

This tracing of a particular story or tradition as it moves through time from one text to another is one of the reasons the Dead Sea Scrolls are so important, particularly for New Testament studies. Older Jewish traditions that appear in both New Testament and Dead Sea texts can be compared and can illustrate the way contemporary Jewish religious movements (the Jesus community and the Qumran community) were developing in the first century. Differing uses of tradition reflect differing religious experiences, and the reverse is also probably true. In any case, critical students of the Bible can ignore neither the way traditions mutate as they are applied anew nor the close connection between the reinterpretation of tradition and religious experience. Both are significant for understanding the dynamic of biblical tradition.

As these many and varied traditions developed, a point arrived when the canonical tradition came to full form and stabilized, giving us the Bible as we know it. In some cases, the process was quite natural and organic. Certain texts, like the Pentateuch, gradually assumed a central role in the life of the community and became sacred and, thus, canonical. In other cases, the process was more mechanical and involved questions about which texts should be included and which ones should not. In the end, a canon, a set of sacred texts, was produced that had its own literary and religious integrity and provided yet another context for these traditions.

For example, although each of the books in the New Testament in some way develops earlier traditions, once the New Testament itself existed as a bounded set of texts, these traditions were again transformed, as early Christians began, for example, to read the Gospels in light of each other and not simply in light of, say, Luke's relationship to Isaiah. As part of the Christian canon, the four Gospels now worked together to form a larger story, a story that moved beyond each Gospel's individual account of Jesus. Likewise, for Christians, the whole of the New Testament was now seen in relation to the Old Testament, an account of prophetic foretelling and a prelude leading up to the stories of Christ's redemptive work. In this larger religious and canonical context, Christians and Jews began to read their common scriptures differently, as Old Testament and as Tanakh. Once again, these different readings were shaped by the respective communities' differing religious and scriptural contexts. And over time, the reading of biblical traditions took on new proportions in light of a concept of canon.

It is important to keep in mind that the development of the biblical tradition did not cease with the actual production of the biblical canon. It continued into what we might call the postbiblical world as well, those times after the texts of the Bible had become authoritative for various religious communities. Even today, the biblical traditions continue to be recontextualized, as new applications of the material are discovered and new associations are generated. Although the text of the Bible itself does not change, the applications of the biblical material shift and the original contexts of the biblical material recede from view.

Streams of tradition flow—changing as the conditions permit and require. The stream may at times be frozen, rock solid, with barely any movement. But that lasts only for a time. Then the thaw comes; the stream begins to flow again; and change resumes its relentless pace. Religious communities are part of tradition streams, and the

Bible for Jews and Christians is a crucial part of their respective traditions, even as these traditions are extended into the present.

Understanding development and change in biblical tradition is a critical component of biblical study. Contexts change, and these changes affect the way tradition and meaning are altered. This is an unfolding process that continues as long as there are communities that consider these traditions to be important. It is this ongoing stream of tradition that links the ancient texts of the Bible with the Jewish and Christian communities of today.

IO

Let's Just
Read It Literally

It is not uncommon to hear someone say, "Let's just read the Bible literally. Let's forget about all this interpretation stuff and just read the Bible for what it says." The impulse for this comment can be appreciated. Serious interpretation of the Bible takes a lot of effort and sustained study, and sometimes in the end all of this effort seems only to work against certain cherished and long-held religious beliefs. Many people want the Bible to sustain them. They do not want to be confronted by strange and new interpretations of it. Others are opposed to the critical study of the Bible because they think God and God's word are beyond human understanding; they can be understood only by the power of the Holy Spirit and not by human reason standing alone. Moreover, such people are concerned that when human beings dig into the scriptures, they, instead of God, seem to become the final arbiter of God's word. These concerns are real, and we ought to make an effort to understand the forces that motivate them.

The Surface Level of the Biblical Text

Even if a person is opposed to studying the Bible critically, the problem of a "literal" reading of biblical material is an issue that is more complicated than might first appear and that will not go away. What makes a reading "literal" as opposed to something else? And is "literality" the same for all types and varieties of texts in the Bible?

In popular usage, "literal" seems to refer to the surface reading of the text, to a straightforward adherence to the face value of the text's wording. But extreme versions of this sense of literality could have strange results. For example, in Mark 12:1–9, Jesus tells a parable about a man who planted a vineyard, put a fence around it, dug a pit for a wine press, built a watchtower, and then rented it to tenants before leaving for another country. When the harvest came, he sent a slave to collect the rent, but the tenants seized and beat him instead of giving him the owner's share of the harvest. Other slaves were sent, and they, too, were beaten or killed. Finally the owner sent his own son, thinking that the tenants would honor him and give him his share of the rent. Instead they seized him, killed him, and threw his body out of the vineyard. A surface level reading of this text would miss the entire point, because this is a parable that takes the form of an allegory. In other words, the characters in the story refer to other figures: God, prophets, Christ, and so on. A meaningful, dare we say a "literal," reading of this text requires more than a close adherence to the surface level of the words. A sound reading would make other judgments about the text; for example, it would be important see that the literary genre of the text is that of allegory.

As the example illustrates, a literal reading of the text cannot be reduced to a surface reading, since judgments about genre, for example, are integral to taking the text at its word, so to speak. In the example, the "correct" and "literal" reading of the text requires that the reader look beneath its surface and recognize the allegorical character of the parable.

If a person were to pick up a novel and read it as history because that is how it presented itself on the surface, the interpretive result would clearly be an unsound reading, according to both the literal character of the text and the intent of the author. If one were to read the seven-day account of creation in Genesis 1 as though it were a primitive scientific explanation of how the world came to be because

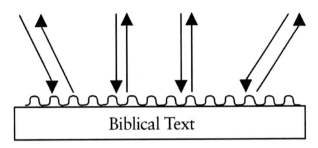

FIGURE 10.1   *The Surface Reading of the Text*

that is how it presents itself on the surface, the interpretive result would be very different, and in fact less literal, than if one read it as a myth designed to speak of something other than the details of how the world came to be. Or, finally, if one were to read the New Testament Gospels as biographies because that is how they appear on the surface, the interpretive result would be quite different, and in fact less literal, than a reading that approached the Gospels as theological narratives.

Of course, to return to the example of the story of the vineyard in Mark, all figurative forms of biblical language are by their very nature not literal in the narrow sense of the term. That is what makes them figurative. However, drawing the line between figurative and nonfigurative language is not always easy and often requires that some interpretive judgments be made. The upshot of this discussion is that even a surface reading of texts requires certain prior interpretive decisions—the decision, for instance, that one is reading history and not fiction, science and not myth, biography and not theological narrative—and to opt for the most obvious choice is often to miss the literal sense of the text. The literal character of any text may not be what it appears to be at first glance. On their surface, the words will not necessarily announce themselves as "history" or "fiction" (it really is possible to mistake a novel for history), and different people will make different initial judgments about how to read the words. Often if those judgments fail to penetrate the surface of the text, then they will also fail to take the text literally.

The Intent of the Biblical Author

As I suggested in passing above, one of the reasons that a literal reading of biblical material cannot be understood simply in terms of the face value of the text is that a truly literal reading will take into account the intent of the author. Some people may say that an author's intentions are always evident in the text. Few people who have thought seriously about this issue would agree, however. I, for one, would contend that there is always a gap between what an author intends and what an author actually produces. If that is true, then the reader who seeks authorial intent will always be making judgments about how to close the gap between what the text appears to say and what was in the mind of the author. Needless to say, this is slippery business and is open to all sorts of legitimate differences of view. To the degree that authorial intent is included in a literal reading of biblical texts, interpretive certainty will be difficult to achieve. A literal reading in that sense will not stem the tide of multiple interpretations of biblical texts; and it will require that numerous interpretive judgments be made.

Paul and his Epistles are a case in point. Scholars are quite certain that Paul actually wrote seven of the New Testament Epistles: Romans, Galatians, 1 and 2 Corinthians, Philippians, Philemon, and 1 Thessalonians. In these Epistles, we have our most direct contact with the mind of Paul and with his intentions. Unlike the book of Acts, in which Luke wrote about Paul, the seven Epistles are primary evidence for the thought and activity of the apostle. Yet if one studies the history of Pauline scholarship, the remarkable differences between various interpretations of Paul become apparent. Many, if not most, of these interpretations claim to represent Paul's thinking. They claim to represent Paul's gospel and his theology. The great diversity of these interpretations points to the fact that trying to discern an author's intention is a very difficult task. No matter how convinced individual scholars may be that their own interpretations accurately represent Paul's mind, the sheer diversity of opinions suggests that seeking to determine authorial intention is no easy matter.

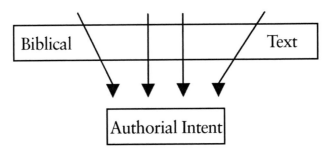

FIGURE 10.2   *Reading for the Intent of the Author*

The Accuracy of the Biblical Text

One of the elements often implicit in surface readings of the Bible is the claim that the Bible is an accurate description of what actually took place at some point in the past. This assertion rests on a prior religious claim that governs all other judgments about the Bible: By definition, the Bible is God's true word and the truth of the Bible is understood in terms of descriptive accuracy. When it says Jonah was swallowed by a whale, Jonah was swallowed by a whale. If it says Jesus exorcised an unclean spirit, he exorcised an unclean spirit. It is that simple. But is it so simple in fact?

Once again, this approach to biblical material can lead to rather questionable readings of texts. If the book of Jonah was never intended to be read as a descriptive account of what took place, why should the reader of Jonah expect the truth of the text to depend on the text's descriptive accuracy? How can that be considered a "literal" reading of the material? As indicated above, readings of texts always involve some decision about literary form or genre, and these judgments affect how one reads literary material. Certainly the truth claims of figurative language cannot always be determined on the basis of the correspondence between this language and some nonfigurative historical reality. That is simply not possible. Moreover, the truth value of a text cannot be reduced to a mere matter of historical accuracy without severely limiting the concept of truth.

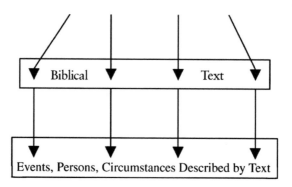

FIGURE 10.3   Reading a Text Assumed to Be Accurate

To illustrate this point, we can use the example of a novel once again. Most novels, according to older systems of classification, are designated as fiction. The reader knows that in most cases the characters never lived and the events never took place. The elaborate plot of the story and the development of the characters are the literary creation of the author. In that sense, the words of the text do not correspond to historical characters and events; the text of the novel is not accurate. Does that mean the novel is not true or has no truth value? Of course not. In the case of a great novel, the truth value of the text may be found in the insight into human experience that is generated as the story line unfolds and the characters develop. Here descriptive accuracy is not a factor of truth. The text may still be true but in quite a different way.

Similar distinctions also need to be made with other forms of biblical literature. The Psalms, for instance, are not examples of descriptive literature, and they may not be forms of literary material where the question of truth is very helpful. Is a poem true? Is a liturgy true? Or a lament? And how would one determine their truth value? In any case, descriptive accuracy cannot be applied as the basis for deciding their truthfulness. The meaningfulness of such biblical texts must be decided on some other basis. The same interpretive requirement is true for many other types of biblical material as well: epistles, prophecies, fables, and apocalypses, to name but a few.

But what about those biblical texts that are ostensibly historical texts? Here the problem of critical historical analysis comes to the fore. Modern critical historians are not willing to accept literary material as historically accurate and reliable simply because the text claims to be so. Such material must be subjected to critical investigation, and corroborating evidence must be supplied when available. The historian then makes critical judgments about the reliability of the evidence and draws his or her own conclusions. The reason these judgments are necessary is that all literary evidence is arranged and told from some perspective; in that sense, all evidence is skewed. The historian must account for this skewing of the evidence, and this account may involve the conclusion that the evidence is not reliable, that it is not descriptively accurate. As a matter of intellectual integrity, the critical historian is obligated to announce this conclusion, if, indeed, that is where the research leads. Critical judgments of this sort apply to both biblical and nonbiblical historical material; and this is the point where critical and noncritical readers of the Bible will probably part company. For those who assert that the biblical materials are descriptively accurate by definition, it is not possible to admit that they are in error. Such an admission would blatantly contradict prior assertions about the text's accuracy. Furthermore, judgments that certain texts are historically inaccurate seem to set human powers of discrimination over and against the word of God.

I began this chapter with a question about what makes a literal reading of the Bible "literal." My goal was not to answer that question but to complicate the issue by proposing that the question of literary genre governs all conceivable ways of reading the Bible literally. A literal reading of the Bible is anything but a simple matter. That much seems certain. For serious students of the Bible, there appears to be no easy way around the complex issues of textual and historical interpretation.

11

What Is Truth?
Fact, Myth,
and Moral Critique

Truth as Historical Correspondence

In Western culture, people absorb quite naturally what can be called a "correspondence" model of truth. In this case, what is true corresponds to something in reality. For example, if a historical account of an event accurately records what took place, it is thought to be true. If what is recounted did not in fact take place, the account is untrue. In other words, what is said to have happened corresponds to what did happen.

A correspondence notion of truth is often brought to the reading of biblical material, and it frequently frames questions of biblical truth. If the text reports the facts of what happened, then the text is true; otherwise it is false. But this is a very limited understanding of both history and truth. History has to do with more than data and evidence. It involves the ordering, arrangement, and interpretation of data and evidence, as well as judgments about the meaning and significance of the evidence. In other words, history is not a mere report of the facts but an interpretive retelling of what happened, what the events mean, and how they are significant. History is how we remember the past, and those remembrances may not always be the same, from person to person or from time to time. It is too simplistic to claim that all notions of historical truth can be reduced to the mere reportage of facts. History is more dynamic than that and thus requires that historians make judgments about what is more important and what is less so. Does the necessity of such judgments mean that there is no such thing as historical truth? Probably not, but it certainly places the discussion in a different frame of reference.

To illustrate the way a historical fact can be invested with meaning and significance, let us think about a specifically Christian claim: Jesus died on a cross for the redemption of the world. This statement contains at least two factual claims: Jesus died, and he died on a cross. The first of these claims is hardly subject to debate, whereas the second is not self-evident and, theoretically, could be tested against the evidence, assuming evidence was available. But both of these claims are rather mundane, to say the least. Not much of significance is at stake in either one. To call the fact of Jesus' death on a cross historical is probably correct but not very unusual.

On the other hand, the claim that Jesus died for the redemption of the world is a monumental claim. It has the potential to be of enormous significance. It is a religious way of investing a historical fact with meaning. This death was not just any death. Others too died on crosses, but this death was special. This one had redemptive significance for the world. Can this claim about the redemptive power of Christ's death be tested against the evidence? Not obviously so. It is difficult to imagine any kind of historical evidence that could substantiate this claim. Does that mean the claim is false? No. It simply means that the truth of any assertion regarding Christ's redemptive death does not rest on sheer historical evidence. When Christians claim that Jesus died on a Roman cross, during the decade when Pontius Pilate was prefect of Judea and Caiaphas was high priest, and, further, that this death redeemed the world, they have fused historical events with theological assertions, and a correspondence model of truth is highly inadequate to judge the truthfulness of such claims.

This example illustrates some of the problems associated with evaluating the truth of biblical material. It points to the fact that truth claims need to be tested according to standards that are appropriate to and commensurate with the kind of claim being evaluated. To do otherwise, even unwittingly, is to mix apples and oranges and can lead to the validation or invalidation of biblical material by fallacious means. To say that something in the Bible is true or false begs for a reply to the question: Relative to what?

Truth by Definition and the Power of Myth

If the correspondence model of truth is not sufficient for the task of determining biblical truth in all its forms, how, then, can we judge the truth of biblical material? One way is what we might call "truth by definition." Many religious people arrive at truth claims by starting with implicit assumptions—certain assertions that are claimed to be true by definition—and then deducing other truth claims from them. For example, Christians claim that Jesus is God's son, by definition. If that is true by definition, then other truth claims can be derived from it by inference and extrapolation. If Jesus is identified as the Son of God, then his teaching, his healing activity on behalf of the sick, his call to discipleship, and his death on the cross somehow also represent the power and presence of God in the world. From the premise that Jesus is God's son, declared to be true by definition, believers can draw these inferences and imagine the kingdom of God breaking into the world in the life and ministry of Jesus. Furthermore, believers can deduce from this truth claim the fact that Christ's life, ministry, and death have significance for their own lives and future salvation. To say that God created the world, or that God forgives sins, or that Christ will come again are further examples of assertions that have been declared to be true by definition ("God is simply like that") and that have then been used as the basis for further inferences about the truth of biblical material.

To speak of "truth by definition" is to speak in a narrow way of a more expansive understanding of truth as something that is relative to a particular cultural worldview. In this case, people begin with basic, deep-seated cultural assumptions that govern the way they look at the world and how they make judgments about truth. Americans, for example, hold dearly to certain notions pertaining to the right to life, liberty, and the pursuit of happiness. These notions are simply part of the fabric of the American worldview; they define what reality is and how it works, and claims about the truth of many of life's issues are made relative to these assumptions, the most fundamental of which are rarely challenged. Different cultures will have different assumptions, but all cultures will assume something. Basic cultural assumptions of this kind are not optional.

I can expand upon the kind of truth that is rooted in a culture's worldview by considering the concept of myth. There are many definitions of the word "myth," but the most common is that it refers to something false; it is an antonym for the word "true." However, people who study and think about the concept of myth do not think of myth as something that is simply false. They have developed many quite sophisticated definitions of myth and studies of how myths function. Since we cannot engage in an extended discussion of these definitions and studies, let me simply offer this summary: Myths are stories that embody the fundamental views of a people about life; they are a record of a people's struggle to understand the world. In this sense of myth, our own culture, no less than the cultures that produced the biblical text, operates within and bases truth claims upon certain mythical notions.

For example, when Americans express their basic conviction that individual human beings have inalienable rights, they are, I submit, reciting American mythology. This myth has been told in countless forms over the years and deals with a fundamental conception of how Americans understand the human person. Geneticists will never find a human gene that identifies a human right. Surgeons will never find an internal body part that contains a human right. The very thought that a "right" could be contained in a gene or an organ strikes us as ridiculous. Nevertheless, many Americans have been willing to fight and die to defend the idea of basic human rights and freedoms. It is an extremely powerful idea that has profound implications for all sorts of claims about human life and social organization. Americans are overwhelmingly committed to the truth of this idea. And yet that truth cannot be established according to a correspondence notion of truth.

There are many examples of biblical myths that function in a similar way. The Israelite idea of "covenant" is one of the most conspicuous. The ancient Israelites believed that they had a special relationship with Yahweh, God. This covenant entailed divine promises and human responsibilities and involved the conviction on the part of the Israelites that a certain piece of real estate, the promised land of Israel, was given to them by God. Like the idea of inalienable rights as it functions in America, the idea of a covenant between God and Israel is clearly a myth, and yet there are Jews to this day who will fight, die, and go to great hardship to live out the implications of the covenant and to occupy the land—because the myth is true. Of course, from the beginning that truth has been relative to a particular cultural perspective. Thus the ancient Canaanites did not, and the modern-day Palestinians do not, abide by that truth; they had and have myths of their own.

The accounts of Jesus' birth in Matthew and Luke are another example of this relationship between myth and truth. A "correspondence" notion of truth would lead one to conclude that these stories are true only if the events and biological facts of the story happened as reported. But if these stories are mythical, something else is going on in them. What could this be? As myths, these are not stories that primarily report events; rather, they probe the deep mysteries of how the divine encounters the human. The divine, God, impregnates a human, Mary, and the tangible result is Jesus Christ, true God and true man. Jesus thus represents the link between the heavenly and the earthly, the mundane and the transcendent.

If the birth stories are myths and not biological and historical reports, does that mean they are untrue? No. But it does mean that truth claims about these stories need to be assessed according to some other standard than historical facticity. The stories are true relative to a basic assumption about the nature of reality: Jesus is the incarnate son of God. As with the myth of the covenant, this truth claim is relative to a particular perspective—in this case, that of Christians—and it is not a claim that all people accept.

There are many biblical themes and stories that fit into these mythical categories. For example, the claim that God created the world and that human beings have dominion over the created order is mythical. This is a powerful idea that may have truth value, but it may not be subject to empirical verification. The idea that Adam and Eve ate of the forbidden fruit, fell from divine favor, suffered the consequences of toil, pain, and enmity, and forever affected the destiny of human beings is another conspicuous mythical idea that may very well be true, and is certainly powerful, but is not subject to empirical verification. Or consider the idea that there will be a final judgment. This claim cannot be verified objectively—unless and until such judgment occurs—but it is a claim that may nonetheless be true relative to certain assumptions about divine justice and activity. Each of these examples illustrates the mythical character of many biblical claims and the way in which the validity and the truth of these biblical statements need to be assessed on some basis other than historical correspondence.

Closely associated with the concept of myth is the concept of ritual. Ritual is not merely the mindless repetition of some human activity. It is the way humans structure their existence relative to certain convictions about the world. It has a shaping and an integrating function in the life of human beings, who use ritual to express their deepest urges and assumptions about their place in the world. Through ritual action, human beings participate in something thought to be integral to existence. For example, the eucharistic (Lord's Supper) texts in the New Testament describe ritual participation in the death of Christ by his adherents. Through bread and wine, consumed in remembrance of Christ's death, the adherents are thought to participate in the very structure of redemptive reality, the death of Christ on the cross: "This is my body. . . This cup . . . is the new covenant in my blood." The body of Christ broken and the blood of Christ shed are not only past-tense realities but present-tense phenomena, as the participants enter into the ritual drama of Christ's death. The eucharistic ritual is not a mere declaration of truth. It is an enactment of truth, according to the

Christian myth of redemption. In this way, myth and ritual work closely together to express truth and to provide a way for the myth's adherents to participate in it.

Biblical Truth and
Moral Critique

Let me make one final observation about the discernment of biblical truth. Discerning the truth of the biblical text will always be a central task for religious communities, as people probe the depths of human experience. But claims about biblical truth, whether those claims speak of truth as correspondence or of the truth of myth and truth by definition, should always be open to critique and evaluation, if critical thinking is to avoid becoming narrow, parochial, and merely self-interested. In my judgment, one particularly valuable stance to take toward biblical truth claims is the stance of moral critique. What social and human consequences have followed from certain historical and religious truth claims? How have these claims played themselves out over time? Are the consequences morally laudable or morally reprehensible? At a minimum, we should ask ourselves about the truth of these claims after we have seen their consequences. For example, when Matthew implies that the blood of Christ is not only on the hands of the Jews in Jesus' day but also on the hands of their descendants, can this statement have any claim to truth, given the way it has contributed to the horrible reality of anti-Semitism? In light of the Christian gospel itself, the consequences of this rather direct Matthean implication seem to be suspect, if not altogether devoid of truth value, that is if the Christian gospel is in fact good news and not bad news. Moral considerations may not finally settle questions of biblical truth; nonetheless, these considerations ought to be part of the interpretive enterprise.

Assessing biblical truth is complicated, and truth in this context cannot be reduced to a single model. The Bible contains multiple levels of meaning and truth, and the critical reader of the biblical texts needs sophistication and flexibility in evaluating all these layers.

Keep in mind, too, that the truth claims of the text emerged from a social and communal context. Likewise, those of us who try to assess them do so in social and communal contexts. In historical and religious matters, truth is social in character, and so is its apprehension. Understanding the social dimensions of truth is important for critical readers of the Bible.

12

This Canon
Has One "N"

Throughout this book, I have made frequent references to the term "canon"; but so far I have offered only sporadic discussion of the concept. In this chapter, I will discuss the process of canonization, the implications of canon, and distinctions between religious and academic contexts for the study of the Bible.

It is clear that the Israelites, Jews, and early Christians produced many more writings than appear in their sacred scriptures. Only a portion of the literature actually written by these people has ended up being part of their sacred library. Although many of these non-biblical books have been preserved, they have never had the standing of the biblical books themselves. What, then, was the process that resulted in the inclusion of some writings into the community's sacred library and the exclusion of others?

Canonization

Here we must distinguish between the Hebrew Bible or Old Testament and the New Testament. The processes of canonization appear to be different in the two cases. The traditional view of the canonization of the Hebrew Bible or the Tanakh holds that the three-fold division of the text was itself the result of the canonization process.

Thus the Torah (the Pentateuch, or first five books), as the most important and authoritative part of the tradition, was put in final form and canonized first, probably sometime during the fifth century B.C. Next the Prophets (Nevi'im), both former and latter, gradually came to be part of Israel's sacred library, though perhaps of somewhat less authority than Torah. Finally, the Writings (Kethuvim), all those books not considered to be part of the Torah and the Prophets, were included. This process was finally brought to an end at the council of Yavneh in 90 A.D., perhaps in response to the rise of the early church with its own emerging body of authoritative literature. In the case of the Writings, there were also debates about whether certain books ought to be included or not. At the end of this process, the Hebrew Bible, with its three-fold division of Torah, Nevi'im, and Kethuvim (thus the designation *Tanakh*) was set. Much later, in the rabbinic period, all of these biblical texts together came to represent the written Torah.

However, this traditional view of the canonization of the Tanakh has been challenged on several fronts. Some scholars have argued against the claim that canonical matters were debated and concluded at Yavneh, and still others have objected to the earlier stages of the process as they are traditionally described. Many different views of the canonization process have been offered in recent years; in the interest of space and by way of contrast, I will suggest only one alternative.

Roger Beckwith, writing in his book entitled *The Old Testament Canon of the New Testament Church,* suggests that by the second century B.C. the Tanakh had a stable structure and that its three sections were not closed at three different times but at two. First the Torah or Mosaic books, those books thought to emanate from Moses, came to be authoritative, in effect canonized, followed by the non-Mosaic books, everything not attributed to Moses. The traditional third section of the Tanakh, that of the Writings, was not really an addition of new material to the two preceding sections but a later subdivision of the non-Mosaic material. Furthermore, the process was thought to be complete by and large before the first century A.D., probably as early as the second century B.C.

According to Beckwith, in the case of the Pentateuch the final Torah material may not have had competitors for inclusion in the sacred library. Rather, new traditions may have been incorporated into this emerging body of national literature, whereas other traditions receded from view and quite naturally disappeared. Hence, it was not really a matter of different books competing against each other for inclusion. A national religious literature was being formed, and the process of formation was gradual. The process played itself out in the way the material was supplemented and shaped internally. Over time, this body of material came to have its own religious authority. It became canonical—the Torah for Jews and eventually part of the Old Testament for Christians.

The canonization process was different for the New Testament, in part because the New Testament documents were written over a much shorter span of time, and in part because they were not a national literature. They were sectarian. They emerged from within different strands of a movement that began as a Jewish sect. Furthermore, the cultural conditions in which early Christianity found itself were quite different from those that contributed to the canonization of the Jewish text. We can catch a glimpse of these conditions by turning to two early Christians who were instrumental in driving the early church to define its sacred body of literature: Marcion and Montanus.

Marcion was a second-century A.D. convert to Christianity who came to the striking theological conclusion that the God of the Jews and of the Jewish scriptures was inferior to the Christian God. The God of the Jews was a God of wrath and vengeance, whereas the God of the Christians was a God of love and mercy. The Jewish scriptures were only a witness to the negative religion from which Christ came to deliver his people. In effect, Marcion argued for the church to sever its theological connection with Judaism and its scriptures, an argument that led him to dismiss not only the Old Testament but also many New Testament texts. In the end, Marcion's canon included only the Gospel of Luke and the Epistles of Paul, purged of all references to the Old Testament.

Marcion's views were rejected as heretical; nonetheless, he forced the early church to consider the extent of its New Testament library.

In rejecting Marcion's position, the church affirmed the authority of other Gospels and Epistles. It kept open the possibility of a larger canon. Unfortunately, the church, in rejecting Marcion's views and defending the integrity of the one God, placed responsibility for divine wrath on the people of Israel, the Jews. If the Old Testament depicted a God of wrath, it was because the Jews had provoked God, and they deserved the punishment they got. The Jews, and not God, were the problem. This view undoubtedly contributed to the rise of anti-Judaism in the early church. The church chose to keep the Jewish scriptures as its Old Testament, but at a significant price.

Also in the second century, Montanus appeared on the Christian scene in Asia Minor, announcing the imminent arrival of the New Jerusalem. The end was near, and the age of the Spirit had arrived, proclaimed Montanus. Along with Maxmilla and Priscilla, two prophetesses who accompanied him, Montanus brought an apocalyptic fervor to his work reminiscent of the first-century church. Claiming the Spirit had spoken to them as it had to the early apostles, the Montanists produced a significant body of literature for which they claimed authority.

The church certainly thought that the Spirit was active in its midst, but had the Spirit spoken to Montanus with the same authority with which it had spoken to Christ's apostles? That was a question that needed to be answered; for if the Spirit had spoken to the Montanists in this way, then their writings could lay claim to being included in the sacred library of the Christians. The church ultimately denied the Montanist claim by asserting that the apostolic period set the standards for understanding future revelation and was to be the norm for the life of the church. Whereas Marcion sought to limit the canon, Montanus sought to open and enlarge it. In response to Marcion, the church was forced to define a concept of the Christian canon, and in response to Montanus the church had to consider the canon's limits. Thus both movements contributed to the formation of the Christian canon.

Other factors also contributed to the formation of the Christian canon, such as the spread of the church and the need for a reliable witness to the testimony of the apostles. The passage of time and the death of the eyewitnesses to Christ's ministry, as well as his failure to return promptly, no doubt contributed to the need for authoritative texts to which the church could turn for guidance. Gradually an authoritative body of literature (Gospels and Epistles) emerged to provide the needed link with the testimony of the apostles. The desire on the part of both Jewish and Christian communities to distinguish themselves from one another may also have contributed to the formation and stabilization of their canons. All of these factors may well have driven the push toward the formation of a Christian canon; but even when the need for a canon became evident, the early Christians still had to decide how to select books for inclusion.

Among the factors that were instrumental in the selection process, two are especially worthy of mention: apostolicity and the rule of faith. The first factor, the claim to apostolic authorship, played a role in the selection of some documents and not others. In response to the Montanists, for example, this type of consideration was clearly important. Closely related to apostolicity was the rule of faith. Does a book represent the faith and tradition of the apostles? Does it represent the faith of the church? If so, it has at least some claim to being included in the canon.

This recourse to the rule of faith indicates that the early church was not only forming a canon but also shaping an orthodoxy (correct belief), and the two processes worked together. The emerging orthodoxy of the early church affected what it would allow to be included in its sacred library and how it would understand the tradition of the apostles. In the end, twenty-seven books were included in the New Testament canon. Many other early Christian writings have been preserved, but only outside the canon. Although these noncanonical books are of enormous historical and religious significance, they have never attained the status of sacred Christian scripture.

Canon as Foundational Text

The facts of the canon's formation do not address sufficiently the larger question of the canon's significance. Once the canon was in place and people turned to these documents for guidance and nour-

TABLE 12.1 Five Different Canons of the Hebrew Bible (Old Testament)

Jewish Tanakh	Roman Catholic Old Testament	Greek Orthodox Old Testament	Russian Orthodox Old Testament	Protestant Old Testament
Torah	*Pentateuch*	*Pentateuch*	*Pentateuch*	*Pentateuch*
Genesis	Genesis	Genesis	Genesis	Genesis
Exodus	Exodus	Exodus	Exodus	Exodus
Leviticus	Leviticus	Leviticus	Leviticus	Leviticus
Numbers	Numbers	Numbers	Numbers	Numbers
Deuteronomy	Deuteronomy	Deuteronomy	Deuteronomy	Deuteronomy
Prophets	*Historical Books*	*Historical Books*	*Historical Books*	*Historical Books*
Joshua	Joshua	Joshua	Joshua	Joshua
Judges	Judges	Judges	Judges	Judges
Samuel	Ruth	Ruth	Ruth	Ruth
Kings	1 and 2 Samuel	1–4 Kingdoms	1 and 2 Samuel	1 and 2 Samuel
Isaiah	1 and 2 Kings	1 and 2 Paralipomenon	1 and 2 Kings	1 and 2 Kings
Jeremiah	1 and 2 Chronicles	1 Esdras	1 and 2 Chronicles	1 and 2 Chronicles
Ezekiel	Ezra	2 Esdras (Ezra-Nehemiah)	2 Esdras (Ezra-Nehemiah)	Ezra Nehemiah
Twelve Prophets	Nehemiah	Tobit	2 and 3 Esdras (Apocryphal)	Nehemiah
Hosea	Tobit	Judith	Tobit	Esther
Joel	Judith	Esther and Additions	Esther and Additions	
Amos	Esther and Additions	1 and 2 Maccabees	1 and 2 Maccabees	*Poetry/Wisdom*
Obadiah	1 and 2 Maccabees			Job
Jonah		*Poetry/Wisdom*	*Poetry/Wisdom*	Psalms
Micah	*Poetry/Wisdom*	Job	Job	Proverbs
Nahum	Job	Psalms and Psalm 151	Psalms and Psalm 151	Ecclesiastes
Habakkuk	Psalms	Prayer of Manasseh	Prayer of Manasseh	Song of Songs
Zephaniah	Proverbs	Ecclesiastes		

Haggai
Zechariah
Malachi

Writings
Psalms
Job
Proverbs
Ruth
Song of Songs
Ecclesiastes
Lamentations
Esther
Daniel
Ezra-Nehemiah
Chronicles

Ecclesiastes
Song of Songs
Wisdom of Solomon
Ecclesiasticus

Prophets
Isaiah
Jeremiah
Lamentations
Baruch and Letter of
    Jeremiah
Ezekiel
Daniel with the
    Prayer of Azariah,
    Song of the Three
    Young Men,
    Susanna, Bel and
    the Dragon
Hosea
Joel
Amos
Obadiah
Jonah
Micah
Nahum
Habakkuk
Zephaniah
Haggai
Zechariah
Malachi

Song of Songs
Wisdom of Solomon
Ecclesiasticus

Prophets
Isaiah
Jeremiah
Lamentations
Baruch and Letter of
    Jeremiah
Ezekiel
Daniel with the
    Prayer of Azariah,
    Song of the Three
    Young Men,
    Susanna, Bel and
    the Dragon
Hosea
Joel
Amos
Obadiah
Jonah
Micah
Nahum
Habakkuk
Zephaniah
Haggai
Zechariah
Malachi

Ecclesiastes
Song of Songs
Wisdom of Solomon
Ecclesiasticus

Prophets
Isaiah
Jeremiah
Lamentations
Baruch and Letter
    of Jeremiah
Ezekiel
Daniel with the
    Prayer of Azariah,
    Song of the Three
    Young Men,
    Susanna, Bel and
    the Dragon
Hosea
Joel
Amos
Obadiah
Jonah
Micah
Nahum
Habakkuk
Zephaniah
Haggai
Zechariah
Malachi

Prophets
Isaiah
Jeremiah
Lamentations
Ezekiel
Daniel
Hosea
Joel
Amos
Obadiah
Jonah
Micah
Nahum
Habakkuk
Zephaniah
Haggai
Zechariah
Malachi

ishment, the character of the church became text-based in much the same way as Judaism, which had centered its life on texts well before Christianity came into existence. In the midst of all the institutional aspects of church life, the church developed an interpretive and literary tradition that was rooted in the Bible and that became foundational for the community's life. That tradition fed the church, and, in turn, the church fed the tradition. The Christian canon, whatever its limits, was a source for divine address, for inspiration and edification, for instruction and theology, and for the church's view of the world. It was one of the things that made the Christian church what it was. Without the Bible, the church would not have been the church as we have come to know it. The Christian canon represents a historical and theological judgment about what the church thought to be important, what the church represented, and how the church would present itself to the world.

Foundational texts function in many different ways for many different kinds of communities. In the legal and political sphere, for example, the American Constitution is a foundational document that governs the way the society organizes itself and observes a system of laws. For most Americans, the Constitution commands respect and allegiance. People turn to it for guidance, and it is reinterpreted to address the problems of the day. Indeed the Supreme Court sits as a supreme interpretive council, rendering judgments on the meaning of the Constitution and adjudicating disputes. Without this document, America would not be America. The Constitution enshrines a part of what makes America the nation that it is. Could the country change its foundational document? Perhaps so, but not without changing who or what it is.

Similarly, the Bible is that kind of document for the Christian church. The books of the Old and New Testaments, now 2,000 years old and more, still have authority for and command the attention of those who claim allegiance to Christ. Christians may differ substantially in their understanding of the Bible and of biblical authority, but virtually all Christians agree that the Bible is a wellspring for the life of the church and its people. Note, however, that outside Christianity the Christian canon does not have this same special status as a source of authority and as an object of reverence. With this thought in mind, let me make an important distinction between the Bible as it belongs to the church and the Bible as it belongs to the historical and intellectual traditions of humanity.

The Church and
the University

From the perspective of the church, it is important to acknowledge both the limits and the intentions of the canon as it has been inherited. For Christians, the Bible is clearly a document of the church, and it speaks to the church. However, when we approach the Bible in an academic context, we operate with a different set of principles. The Christian canon may be the product of decisions that the early church made about, for instance, the rule of faith, but those decisions do not govern the study of the Bible in an academic context. In this context, the critical search for truth is the goal, not the theological edification of the faithful. To draw the distinction sharply, there is a profound difference between the theology of the church and the academic work of the university. The church and the university work out of different interpretive contexts and aim toward different goals. The church serves the faith and life of the religious community, whereas the university seeks to generate new insight into these traditions for the sake of human thought and knowledge.

Although this distinction is important and ought to be observed, it is not the case that the church and the university are irrevocably opposed to each other. They can and ought to be in dialogue. They should be able to learn from one another. And when they are at odds with one another, they should seek to understand the basis of their differences. Confusing these two contexts and these two purposes, however, often leads beginning students of the Bible to think rather imprecisely about the modes of interpretive analysis and the objectives of the critical study of the biblical texts.

Although the church and the university have been closely connected historically in Western culture, they are quite distinct in the modern world. In some ways this is unfortunate for both. In other ways, the differences between these two institutions represent important conceptual distinctions concerning the limits and the modes of human knowledge. The critical study of the Bible frequently brings these issues to the fore, and the concept of canon is close to the center of this discussion.

13

The Three Legs of Interpretation

The Bible is self-evidently a public book. By that I mean that people with different interests read it for quite different purposes. The Bible is legitimately open to anyone who wants to read it, for whatever purpose; it is not strictly the domain of religious communities. Some people read the Bible because they are interested in history or literature; others find it interesting as a record of ancient religious beliefs.

Even within Jewish and Christian religious communities as such, people frequently read the Bible for different purposes. Within these communities, some people read it out of devotion, to nourish their spiritual lives; others are interested in the liturgical role of scripture, the way it fits into the worship life of the individual and the community. Clergy work closely with the Bible in sermon preparation, and literally millions of people hear sermons preached on biblical texts each week. Members of Jewish and Christian communities also read the Bible for consolation in the midst of illness and personal suffering. The Bible as God's word sustains and builds up the faithful in the midst of travail. Furthermore, anyone who has studied the theological legacy of either Judaism or Christianity knows that biblical texts have played an enormous role in the shaping of both traditions.

Indeed, the interests and purposes that people bring to their readings of the Bible are many and varied. The Bible is truly a public book open to all. And yet amid the myriad readings of this public text, we can identify three aspects of the interpretive process that all readings of the Bible have in common. It is the purpose of this chapter to outline briefly these three legs of interpretation and their importance for any truly public examination of the Bible.

Constituency

The first leg of interpretation is the matter of *constituency*—the group of people who share enough of a common interest or purpose to read the Bible together. The concept of constituency is not precise; groups of people who share common interests or purposes are not always clearly identifiable. Nonetheless, the concept of constituency serves to remind us that biblical interpretation is a social phenomenon. Thus people who share common interests in reading the Bible often speak to one another about their interpretations and contribute to each other's understanding of the text. They often congregate into communities of like-minded readers, and they pursue the interpretation of the Bible for the purpose of expressing their interests.

For example, peasant people in Latin America often gather around the Bible to hear words of encouragement that might sustain them in their circumstances of poverty and oppression. They read the biblical texts as a way of challenging their oppressors, as a part of their resistance to the injustices that have been inflicted upon them. In these moments of challenge, they form a reading community: They share a common interest in the text, a common purpose for reading the text, and a sense that the text addresses them and their circumstances.

In a very different way, academic experts also form a reading community. They share a common scholarly interest in the biblical texts. This community may be fleeting, and, to be sure, its boundaries are not clear, but for a time people gather together around the biblical text, sharing not only a common interest but a common way of reading. Unlike the community of peasants in Latin America, the social bonds of this community are loose; scholars may be in physical proximity to one another only infrequently, and in the electronic age this community may even be virtual. Still, common interests and purposes, if not immediate social bonds, unite scholars into a reading community.

In a still different sense, individuals who read the Bible privately do so, perhaps unbeknownst to themselves, as part of a reading community, or at least as part of a historic tradition and an intellectual legacy. We may not wish to describe this tradition or legacy as a constituency or a community, but it is clear that individuals are influenced by larger social, religious, and intellectual forces. It is impossible for a modern American, even a modern American locked away in a closet, to read the Bible in a vacuum. Even the most private of readers cannot escape the views of modern science, or of North American individualism, or of a capitalistic economic system, and the ways in which these cultural phenomena impinge upon how one reads the biblical text.

The notion of constituency puts into a different frame of reference the common refrain: "Everyone interprets the Bible in his or her own way." The implication of this refrain, to overstate the case, is that biblical interpretation is a highly idiosyncratic exercise in which each person does his or her own thing, producing conclusions out of little more than the imagination, with little or no debt to anyone or any thing else. I do not mean to deny the role of human imagination and creativity in the interpretive process, but what impresses me most about the biblical interpretations that I read, especially those of my students, is that they are heavily influenced by the communities, traditions, and social legacies that have shaped them.

Of course, most students, and most people generally, have their own interests (or disinterests) that come into play in their readings of biblical material. In this sense, reading the Bible is an individual affair, but, as far as I am concerned, it is far from individualistic. The social, religious, and intellectual factors that shape one's questions and interpretive line of sight are extremely important aspects of interpretation, and they should always be of interest to the critical student of the Bible. Knowing about these factors is an important feature of being an effective interpreter.

Location

The second leg of interpretation is the matter of *location*. Where are people when they read the Bible? Are they in a lecture hall at the University of Oxford? Are they part of a Wednesday morning community Bible study in a nice house in a suburb of a major American city? Are they at a Catholic funeral service? Or are they in a hospital room as a Protestant pastor ministers to a convalescing cancer patient?

As these questions have already implied, location is not simply a matter of where readers are (a lecture hall, a house, a church, a hospital) but also a matter of what sort of people have congregated in this place. Are the readers well fed and clothed, upwardly mobile and professionally successful? Or are they blue-collar workers in a mining community? Or are they oppressed, hungry, and largely uneducated black South Africans in a township of Johannesburg? Location is a matter not only of geography but also of social circumstance—it is what we might call social location, and it is always significant, for as many scholars have shown, one's vantage point governs what one sees.

One of the most interesting aspects of this leg of interpretation is that readers' locations shift from time to time. Thus modern people find themselves reading the Bible in different locations, at different times, under different social circumstances, with different interests—in short, their vantage of the world and of the text changes. Some people move from religious unbelief to belief, or from belief to unbelief. Others move from wealth to poverty or from oppression to liberation or from socialism to capitalism. Perhaps even more poignantly, some people operate in many different locations all in the same day. Clergy, for example, may read the Bible with a patient in the hospital, teach a Bible class at someone's home, give a sermon in church, and turn to the Bible as part of a devotional routine—all in one day. Clearly, in this example the reader's location has shifted from one activity to the next.

Such shifts of location can be especially troublesome for people who begin the serious academic study of biblical material after having come out of particular locations within the church that seem at odds with critical biblical scholarship. This kind of shift in location, which entails new procedures for reading and thinking about the Bible, can result in a profound sense of dislocation. The appearance of the text in the classroom may be quite different from its appearance within a faith community of like-minded believers. Students cannot help but bring their past histories with them into the classroom, and these past experiences with the biblical text often make it difficult for them to adjust to a new set of interpretive procedures and rules of discourse.

Interestingly, a vast number of students arrive in the classroom with no past experience of the text, or of academic life. But these students, no less than those who arrive from a community of faith, also suffer from a sense dislocation, which simply proves the point that any shift in location makes demands on the reader, and the process of relocating oneself can take time and be disconcerting for many serious-minded people.

The ability to adjust to these kinds of dislocation is an important aspect of biblical interpretation, but, more broadly, it has also become an important feature of modern life. In a rapidly changing world, with all of its technological marvels, changing social systems, and cultural confrontations, the flexibility to adjust and to relocate both physically and intellectually is a necessary capacity. In the absence of this capacity, people often pull back from the world and refuse to engage it because it frightens them. Or sometimes they lose their mental and social equilibrium and expend enormous amounts of energy just trying to cope and remain human in the face of an impersonal world.

The Bible and the religious traditions that stem from it have historically played a prominent role in keeping people rooted and oriented in a changing world. If that role is to continue in the fast-paced world that faces us at the dawn of the twenty-first century, then people will have to develop the critical capacity—the interpretive flexibility—to shift locations without sacrificing conviction. This capacity, this habit of mind and heart, is an attribute to be prized in all facets of life, and the study of the Bible is one of the ways that people can develop it.

Function

The third leg of interpretation is the matter of *function*. If constituency and location pertain to the "who" and the "where" of biblical interpretation, then function deals with the "how." There is no doubt that each of these three legs is closely related to the other (thus to speak of "social location," as I did above, is to speak of "who" and "where" at the same time), but the question of function is somewhat different than the other two. It focuses on the means and methods of reading, as shaped by the interests and purposes of a constituency and the vantage point of a particular reader.

Consider, for example, the difference between the Bible's liturgical function and its historical function. When it is used for liturgical purposes in the context of worship, the Bible functions to represent the word of divine address and focuses the individual voices of the community into a common voice of praise and prayer. On the other hand, when the Bible is used for historical purposes, it functions as evidence of past events and is thus subjected to the rules of rational and logical argumentation. Obviously, the function of the Bible as historical evidence is a far cry from its function as divine address in the liturgy; and both of these functions are quite different from the function of the Bible as artistic expression, as literature or poetry. Thus without taking into account the function of a particular biblical text at a given moment, the serious reader cannot make any final decision about what the text means.

To ignore the issue of *function,* just as to ignore *constituency* and *location,* is to run the risk of seriously misusing the Bible, or at least of using it poorly, all the while creating an interpretive muddle. Self-consciousness in these matters is crucial for keeping one's balance in the face of religious and interpretive chaos. Serious and educated readers of the Bible have to make clear distinctions between the different constituencies, the different locations, and the different functions that bear upon various readings of the biblical text.

With those distinctions in hand, readers can begin to negotiate their way through the complexity of the Bible, and of the religious communities for which it is a foundational text, with intellectual integrity. In the absence of these distinctions, the Bible and religion too easily become sources for division and disagreement. Often, but not always, such disagreement is submerged under the illusion that religion and the Bible are merely private matters and that we dare not speak of them publicly, for to do so would cause the divisions to spill out into the open—and someone might end up being offended.

"Each to their own" thus becomes the language of toleration in the face of difference. But by locking the Bible and religion just beneath the surface of our social lives, right alongside the reality of religious divisions and fears, this language perpetuates the façade that the Bible and religion are private matters that cannot be examined in public light. But left under the surface of public discourse, the biblical text and the divisions and fears that accompany its interpretation operate in the dark shadows of the unexamined life. And in the sphere of religion, that is a volatile situation.

14

A Question
of Purity

Experience with American college students, for the most part from Protestant Christian orientations, tells me that the popular conception of religion has two general features: Religion is a system (1) of beliefs and (2) of ethics, of right and wrong. This perception is not necessarily incorrect; but when it is applied to the Judaisms of the second temple period (520 B.C. to 70 A.D.) and to the biblical traditions that spring from them certain distortions can result. This chapter is devoted to one of the features of biblical religion that cannot simply be reduced to belief and ethics: the ritual matter of religious purity and impurity.

Many forms of Judaism during the second temple period were strongly influenced by notions of purity and by the ritual mechanisms designed to restore it when defilement occurred, which it invariably did. Purity was more than a simple matter of belief and ethics; it constituted an overarching view of how the world was organized, how it operated, and what ritual order was necessary to maintain the world in right relationship with God. Most modern Christians, and Jews for that matter, do not think of their religion in terms of purity and the rituals that restore it when it is lost; but many early Jews and Christians did. Thus if we want to understand the nature of these early religious traditions and the biblical legacy they left in their wake, then we must seek to understand something about purity as a factor in biblical religion.

The Rise of Judaism

With the final destruction of Jerusalem and of Solomon's temple by the Babylonians in 586 B.C., the history and religion of the Israelite people took a new direction. Many of the Israelites were relocated to the heart of the Babylonian empire and were forced to adapt themselves and their religion to the changed circumstances of life in exile. Responding to the question "Why has this happened to us?" the exiles concluded that they had sinned against God and were being punished for their transgressions. As a consequence of this conclusion, they set about consolidating and reshaping their sacred traditions, organizing their life around the sanctification of daily activity, and seeking to fulfill the dictum "You shall be holy, for I the Lord your God am holy" (Leviticus 19:2). With these developments, the seeds of early Judaism were sown.

In the period that followed, a structured worldview, a ritual way of life, a concept of Torah, and eventually a rebuilt temple would come to shape much of Jewish life. Infusing this developing system of Judaism was a notion that cleanness was tantamount to purity and purity was tantamount to holiness. Thus for many Jews, especially those who lived close to the second temple, the issue of purity was of concern and affected the organization of their entire way of life. Figure 14.1 illustrates the structure of this Israelite world.

The figure depicts a structure of holiness that radiates from the center. Although we must not overstate the rigidity of this structure, nor its applicability throughout Israel, it nonetheless expresses a central aspect of the worldview we encounter in the biblical text. Everything has its place; and when everything is in its place, the world is in equilibrium. When that balance is disrupted, when impurity enters the system, the proper order is violated, and harmony (purity) must be restored.

Purity or impurity in this world was evident in various ways. Boundaries, for instance, were important—the boundaries between

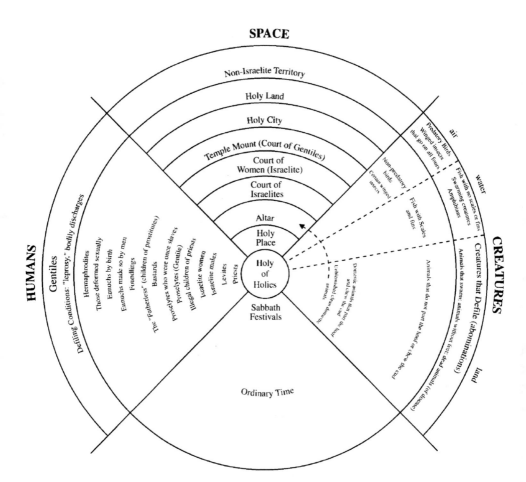

SPACE

Non-Israelite Territory

Holy Land

Holy City

Temple Mount (Court of Gentiles)

Court of Women (Israelite)

Court of Israelites

Altar

Holy Place

Holy of Holies

Sabbath Festivals

Ordinary Time

air

water

land

CREATURES

Creatures that Defile (abominations)

Predatory Birds

Winged insects that go on all fours

Fish with no scales or fins

Non-predatory birds

Certain winged insects

Swarming creatures

Amphibians

Fish with Scales and fins

Animals that swarm; animals without feet; dead animals (of disease)

Animals that do not part the hoof or chew the cud

Unblemished clean animals

Domestic animals that part the hoof and chew the cud: the food animals

HUMANS

Gentiles

Defiling Conditions: "leprosy," bodily discharges

Hermaphrodites

Those deformed sexually

Eunuchs by birth

Eunuchs made so by men

Foundlings

The "Fatherless" (children of prostitutes)

Bastards

Proselytes who were once slaves

Proselytes (Gentile)

Illegal children of priests

Israelite women

Israelite males

Levites

Priests

TIME

FIGURE 14.1   An Israelite Priestly View of the World

Jew and Gentile, between one type of animal and another, between the sick and the healthy, between the dead and the living. To breach such boundaries was to move from purity to impurity, from being clean to being unclean, from being normal to being abnormal. Of course, it was impossible not to breach certain boundaries fairly frequently, hence the careful delineation of boundaries was accompanied by an elaborate system of prescriptions and rituals that established protocols for breaching and then restoring boundaries.

Consider Matthew 8:1–4, which records the story of a leper who is healed by Jesus. In the course of the exchange between the two men, the leper requests to be made clean. After Jesus heals him with the words "Be made clean," he says to the leper, "show yourself to the priest, and offer the gift that Moses commanded as a testimony to them." Clearly the issue of purity is central to this story and affects the way the two men respond to each other. Thus physical infirmity, as "abnormality," is cast in terms of cleanness and uncleanness. Also central to the story is the related issue of boundaries. To be a leper in Jesus' day was to be cast across the outer boundary of the community—it was to be, quite literally, an outcast. To be made clean in this case is thus to be allowed back across that boundary into the community—and such a crossing requires ritualized clearance. For this reason Jesus sends the now cleansed leper to the priest.

"Matter" out of Place

Cultural anthropologists operate with a definition of "dirt" that is helpful at this point. They define "dirt" as matter that is out of place. Earth found in a field is soil, but earth that has sifted into a house in a storm or has been tracked across the living room carpet is "dirt." It is out of its proper place. Likewise, in the example from Matthew, the deviation from the physical norm is described in terms of uncleanness. The leper's bodily matter is not configured the way it is supposed to be. It is unclean. When the structural order of things is violated, things become "dirty," contaminated by their deviation from the norm.

The temple as it was reconstituted after the return of the exiles from Babylon was especially vulnerable to defilement. Only certain priests had the right to enter the holiest precincts of the temple; if anyone else entered these precincts they would defile the sacred space, which would then have to be rededicated to its proper place and function in the structure of things. By extension, the whole priestly and sacrificial system in Jerusalem was filled with ritual purity considerations. Even to this day, there appear in Jerusalem the remains of ritual baths *(mikvoth)* that were used by priests and pilgrims in rites of purification associated with the temple and the priestly caste.

These baths may also have been used to purify women following child birth and menstruation. At least some people in Israel thought that these biological events rendered women unclean until certain specified periods of time had passed. Concerns about purity thus extended into the most basic aspects of life. Even food—what could be eaten and how it was prepared—was a matter of purity. In the world of Judaism, purity was a serious concern—especially to those Jews who had priestly sensibilities—and it could affect a person's status in the social and religious ordering of life.

The full meaning of many of the stories about Jesus that we encounter in the Gospels comes to light only against the background of this Jewish concern with boundaries and purity. For example, Jesus brought the wrath of the religious authorities on himself by implying that he could forgive sins. When the authorities charged him with blasphemy—with usurping the prerogatives that belong to God alone—and sought to do away with him, they in effect accused Jesus of breaching boundaries and of not minding his place in the order of things. Jesus' associations with the unclean, with tax collectors, prostitutes, and sinners, as well as his exorcisms of unclean spirits, also played themselves out against a background of priestly purity concern. It is quite likely that Jesus was considered problematic by at least some people in his day (perhaps by those with strong priestly concerns) precisely because he seemed to be an exception to the normal order of things.

On the other hand, it would not be accurate to conclude that Jesus stood against all of Judaism's legalistic purity concerns. Such a portrait of Jesus is often used to portray Christianity as superior to Judaism. But the reality of Jesus' relationship to the purity codes is much more complex. Thus stories in the Gospels that portray Jesus as someone who performed objectionable activities on the Sabbath, or that portray his disciples as eating with unwashed hands, may reflect the concerns of the gospel writers and the early church as much as or more than they do the concerns of Jesus himself.

One of the indications that Jesus' views about purity were complex is the fact that his followers continued to argue about the role of these concerns in the fledgling Christian communities. Had Jesus simply dismissed all of Judaism's legalistic purity concerns, there would have been little doubt that his followers should do likewise; or if Jesus had simply accepted these concerns as his own, then, again, his followers would have not had much to argue about. For Paul, however, writing more than twenty years after Jesus' death, the issues of whether Jewish Christians should eat with Gentile Christians or whether they should eat meat that had been previously offered to idols were unsettled purity issues of urgent concern. Eating meat that had previously been offered to idols raised all sorts of questions about purity. Did eating food offered to idols violate the Ten Commandments? Did it violate Torah? Did it render one unclean?

Paul was also concerned about the related issue of circumcision—which was one of the ways that Jews marked the boundary between their community and the world of the Gentiles. By relativizing the need for circumcision and arguing for a church made up of both Jews and Gentiles, Paul was surely pushing the limits of a traditional first-century Jewish worldview. Thus it is not surprising that his views were so controversial, indeed objectionable, to many of his Jewish contemporaries. But, again, it would not be accurate to conclude that Paul stood against the Jewish notion of purity as such. Rather, at the bottom of Paul's missionary work was an attempt to structure a new view of the world with a new understanding of what was religiously acceptable and "pure." In Paul's view, God had acted anew in Christ; Jews remained the chosen people, but Gentiles were now to be included in the community, which Paul referred to as the body of Christ.

Unlike Paul and Jesus and other first-century Jews, most people today do not think about religion in terms of clean and unclean, pure and impure. To think critically about the Bible and the religious world out of which the biblical texts emerged thus requires that we make a special effort to step into a world where many of the most important aspects of existence were linked to an overarching concern with purity.

Of course, we moderns have our own underlying ideas about how the world is put together and about the boundaries that keep everything in its proper place. And if we take seriously the insights of cultural anthropologists that "dirt" is simply a way of naming things that are out of place, then it is clear that we, too, operate with notions of clean and unclean, even if we do not use those terms. Think of the social outcasts of our own culture—the homeless, AIDS patients, or racial minorities, for example—and of the way they are often portrayed as "dirty." Such people, who in one way or another are "out of place," are no doubt acutely aware that the modern world has its own boundaries and its own understandings of purity. One of the benefits of a serious attempt to understand how purity functioned in the biblical world is that such an attempt can be a catalyst for thinking about how issues of purity and cleanness continue to inform our own views of how the world is put together.

15

Digging in the Text
and in the Dirt

There is a substantial difference between studying literary texts and studying material remains, material artifacts from past cultures. Literature has its own peculiar character, as do material artifacts; thus the work of biblical interpretation is clearly not the same as the work of biblical archaeology. With notable exceptions, biblical scholars and archaeologists have often lived in their own academic worlds and have gone their separate scholarly ways.

When these two worlds have converged, it has often been the case that archaeology has been used, or might we say co-opted, to substantiate the historical record of the Bible. Naturally many archaeologists are uneasy about this use of their craft, because it raises the issue of whether archaeological findings are being directly or indirectly skewed to support the Bible. Furthermore, these same archaeologists argue against the very notion of "biblical archaeology," preferring to speak instead of the "archaeology of the Middle East" or the "archaeology of Syro-Palestine." They argue that the Bible represents only one aspect of ancient Middle Eastern culture, and it is a mistake to think that this single text should guide the work of archaeologists in the region. Understandably, then, many archaeologists have been reluctant to get too close to traditional biblical scholarship.

On the other hand, when biblical scholars have shown an interest in the reconstruction of biblical history, they have usually exhibited a bias in favor of literary evidence and literary sources, which means that the work of archaeologists has been of only tangential interest.

In recent times, this state of affairs seems to be changing, if only slightly. Working solely within the parameters of their own craft, archaeologists have been able to show that their findings are important for the work of reconstructing biblical history and for understanding biblical texts. Likewise, students of biblical literature are coming to see that the work of archaeologists has something valuable to contribute to the work of critical biblical study, apart from the earlier attempts simply to substantiate the truth and authority of the Bible.

In both fields of investigation, new methods of analysis have opened fresh ways of understanding the world out of which the biblical material emerged. In some cases, for example, the recent interest in social history and cultural anthropology among biblical scholars has disposed the respective disciplines toward each other. If one is interested in the social history of a particular biblical period or place, it is rather difficult to ignore the findings of the archaeologists who have excavated the relevant sites. And if one is interested in piecing together the material record of a particular site, it may well be important to know the latest analysis of any literary texts that pertain to the site.

These signs that biblical scholars and archaeologists have common interests are encouraging, and we can only hope that these interests continue to converge and that scholars in both fields continue to work together for the mutual benefit of biblical scholarship and archaeology. In any event, the purpose of this chapter is to introduce students to each of these disciplines in order to outline what is at stake in the relationship between them.

Textual Material

All texts occupy a certain position in the social scheme of things. Most obviously, they are produced by people who can write, and they are read by people who can read. This may not seem like a significant observation in the context of the modern developed world,

but in the context of the world of ancient Israel it takes on importance. Some scholars estimate that during the time of Jesus the illiteracy rate in Israel was 97 percent. That figure serves to remind us
that the biblical texts emerged out of and functioned within a very
small segment of the Jewish population.

Illiterate people, of course, would have been exposed to these texts
second hand, that is, they would have heard others reading them or
talking about what they contained, but the people who actually
worked with textual material first hand came from a narrow slice of
the society. Thus, to the extent that texts reflect the circumstances of
their authors, the biblical texts represent a very narrow range of social and religious interest, that of an elite. Although the implications
of this observation can be overdrawn, they should not be dismissed
out of hand. Literary and textual evidence is undoubtedly important
for historical reconstruction; without it historians could not do their
work. But historians need to account for the peculiarities of literary
material when they use it for historical work.

For example, when historians read the legal material in Leviticus,
should they conclude that these prescriptions are reflective of the
way things were actually carried out in ancient Israel? Or does the
material simply reflect how someone, perhaps a priestly elite,
thought things ought to be done? To take another example, does
Luke's account of Paul in the book of Acts describe what the apostle
did and said? Or does it reflect the theological agenda of Luke regarding Paul and his mission to the Gentiles? And if it is some of
both, how does one separate the historical record from Luke's theological claims? Both of these examples illustrate the problem associated with literary evidence. It is material circumscribed by an author's intentions, and that intentionality must be accounted for,
especially when literature is used as historical evidence. Of course,
discerning an author's intentions is not an easy task; it may even be
impossible, particularly when the author has made an effort to con-
ceal things in the text. Nonetheless, the task remains an important
part of the interpretive process, and its difficulty simply reminds us
that textual material is not always transparent, and that sometimes
discerning an author's intentions requires great care and skill.

Metaphorical and imaginative language also complicates the work of historians who work with literary evidence. First historians must decide if the language of a particular text is metaphorical and figurative? Is it imaginative or descriptive? Because modern readers are so far removed from the context in which the literature was produced, it is not always easy to determine whether or not the language of an ancient text is imaginative or descriptive. Indeed, there is sometimes a tendency to read figurative language literally and imaginative language as somehow historically descriptive. Once historians have decided that a text is metaphorical and imaginative, then they have to decide if such language reveals anything of historical interest.

Archaeological Material

The evidence unearthed by archaeologists often gives us a rather direct look into the everyday life of ancient peoples. By digging through layers of dirt and remains, archaeologists create a window that provides historians with a view of the ancient world. Archaeologists give us glimpses into the way people lived, how they organized their lives, what kinds of technology they had developed, how they expressed themselves in art and design, as well as into the way goods and peoples seem to have moved from place to place and interacted with one another.

For example, archaeologists digging at the site of the ancient city of Sepphoris, an important Galilean city only a few miles from Nazareth, have provided important information about life in ancient Galilee during the time of Jesus. And the dig at Kefar Nahum (Capernaum) has unearthed interesting information about life in the community where Jesus started his ministry. Some people have even asserted that the apostle Peter's house can be identified at Kefar Nahum. Be that as it may, the site provides important information about how people organized their living arrangements and conducted their everyday affairs in that village during the time of Jesus and after.

Jerusalem is also a storehouse of ancient remains and unearthed artifacts from many different periods in the city's 3,000-year history.

One can see remains from the times of ancient Israel, from the temple that Herod built in the first century B.C., from a house inhabited by a wealthy priestly family in the upper city dating from the first century A.D., and so on. The archaeological evidence in Jerusalem is massive, and it provides a wealth of information for historians and students of the Bible.

Even beyond the borders of Israel, other countries of the eastern Mediterranean and the Middle East contain their own archaeological treasures and in some cases supply important contextual material for understanding the world of the Bible. Of course, the full value of such treasures is evident only after archaeologists have interpreted them. As with literature, this interpretive task is not always easy, but material evidence presents a quite different set of challenges.

The material evidence that archaeologists unearth is, broadly speaking, of two kinds: inscriptional and noninscriptional. Some inscriptional evidence, like the texts found at Qumran (Dead Sea Scrolls) and Nag Hammadi (Gnostic texts), is literary in nature. Obviously, material of this sort presents archaeologists with the problems of interpretation that I outlined in the previous section. Such literary finds are rare, however. In most cases, archaeologists discover inscriptional evidence of a different sort—such things as commercial transactions, legal materials, or ceremonial inscriptions. This kind of archaeological evidence often helps establish dates and contains information about common, "down to earth" matters of life and culture. As with all written material, interpreters must be alert to any peculiarities of the evidence; but because the purpose of such documents was often bureaucratic and not literary, these peculiarities are not usually the result of the distorting effects of an author's intentions.

Like its nonliterary inscriptional counterpart, noninscriptional material does not bear the distortions of an author. Rather, it is in some sense "unintended" material—the "left overs" of a culture—and any distortion that accompanies it is the result of precisely this "unintended" character. Archaeologists dig through layers of remains from different periods left by ancient peoples as they built and rebuilt their communities. These remains can be a jumble, difficult to

FIGURE 15.1   *View of Ancient Sepphoris*

FIGURE 15.2   *Synagogue Remains at Kefar Nahum*

FIGURE 15.3   *Cave Near Khirbet Qumran*

FIGURE 15.4   *Temple Mount, Jerusalem*

untangle and interpret. Making sense of them is certainly not arbitrary, but it is clearly not a precise science either. Hence, the process of interpretation and revision among archaeologists is as critical to the study of material remains as is the study of literary material among biblical scholars.

Biblical Scholars and
Archaeologists in Conversation

Used in conjunction with literary texts, the material artifacts can help us understand how the vast majority of ordinary people lived in the ancient world of the Bible. With the careful work of the archaeologist leading the way, we can learn about the concrete circumstances that shaped the lives of the people who wrote the Bible, the people who are featured in it, and the people who used it. By understanding the work of archaeologists and paying attention to their conclusions, biblical scholars are given a plumb line against which to check their conclusions about biblical history and biblical texts. This plumb line can prevent scholarly self-deception and intellectual dishonesty. The work of archaeologists in some cases may confirm the results of textualists; in others it may disconfirm them; but in all cases it will cast light on the historical reconstructions of people who rely on literary evidence, especially if their concern is for the social and material aspects of culture.

Of course any light that archaeology casts on the biblical text, and vice versa, will be a theory-laden light. Regardless of the type of evidence that might be used to inform a historical reconstruction, this evidence must invariably be assembled and interpreted according to some pattern or manner of presentation. Theories about how cultures are formed, organize themselves, and actually work are an important part of interpreting both textual and material evidence. If archaeologists and biblical scholars sometimes have difficulty conversing with one another, it is, no doubt, not only because one group of scholars digs in texts and the other group digs in the dirt, but also because their interpretations of the evidence are rooted in different theories. It seems to me that questions about theory give textualists and archaeologists something important to talk about.

Students who want to pursue the ongoing conversation between archaeologists and biblical scholars would do well to start by studying maps and learning the relative locations of various places in Israel and environs. In addition, students can consult the audio-visual and interactive computer resources that are increasing all the time and that provide a graphic portrayal of the biblical world. Popular but good periodicals that deal specifically with biblical archaeology are also available. *Biblical Archaeology Review*, for example, provides a good overview of current developments in the field. Finally, however, there is nothing quite like traveling to Israel, Asia Minor, and Greece, walking the sites, and looking at the remains that have been unearthed. When the opportunity to go to these lands presents itself, *do not* pass up the chance to see them in person!

16

The Bible and
the Examined Life

In formal settings, biblical study usually takes place at introductory levels of instruction. In college classrooms across the country, students take biblical classes, usually at an introductory level, as part of their humanities or liberal arts curriculum. Most of these students probably do not have any real interest in majoring in religion or going into professional religious work. But many may well have an interest in biblical material and the issues raised by the study of the Bible for intellectual and personal reasons. Opening the world of biblical study to inquiring minds at the introductory level is certainly as challenging and stimulating for teachers as pushing back the frontiers of biblical scholarship in a graduate school. And for students in introductory classes, the exposure to rich and powerful material that often links up with great existential concerns can be captivating, invigorating, and sometimes unsettling. Perhaps above all, students in these classes have the opportunity to confront specific historical, literary, and religious issues while at the same time seeking to make connections with other aspects of human knowledge and experience.

It is precisely in these introductory courses that the hooks are often set for those who will eventually end up pursuing further study of the Bible, religion, or theology. These initial experiences are crucial, for they give most of us our first formative look at the field.

They are learning moments that pique the imagination and stimulate curiosity. Virtually everyone who goes on to study biblical material more thoroughly, whether in seminary or graduate school, passes through the introductory phases of biblical study, where skills of analysis and interpretation are first forged. More often than not, students are coming to the study of the Bible with little or no exposure to the material prior to their first classroom experience. The Bible is not part of home life and culture the way it once was. Religious searching may be a conspicuous part of modern life, but for many people the religious disciplines of Bible reading and study are not. Increasingly, even seminaries have found that they are required to do more and more introductory work themselves because of the general level of their students' unfamiliarity with the material. It is with this increasing importance of introductory biblical studies classes in mind that I turn my attention in this chapter to the overarching task of introducing students to the Bible.

Introductory Courses, Old and New

There was a time when critical biblical study at the initial stages was thought to involve deconstructing, disassembling, and, in some cases, correcting what students had already been taught and brought with them into the classroom. Even under the circumstances that prevailed in the past, the value of that procedure can be questioned, but today that approach is largely irrelevant for most students. Most students simply do not come to class with anything to deconstruct or disassemble. I say this without fixing blame, but with the full recognition that the immediate circumstances of our culture shape the tasks of teaching and learning in an increasingly postbiblical world. Although there may be much in this state of affairs to lament, I suspect that if we apply our imaginations and energy to these circumstances, new and interesting possibilities for the critical study of the Bible will emerge in their own right. In this brief section, I want to address some of these possibilities.

Traditionally, introductory biblical courses have come in many forms. Sometimes they have taken a survey approach to the material; at other times certain bodies of biblical literature, say the Torah or the Prophets, have been the primary focus of attention. Sometimes introductory courses have highlighted religious and theological themes that can be traced throughout the canonical material; at other times they have placed the Bible in the context of the historical study of religion as a phenomenon of human life. But almost always, historical and literary study has provided the backbone of traditional introductory courses.

Hence, introductory courses have often focused on such things as the historical communities that produced the texts, the stages through which the texts have gone in the process of formation, the way different communities have read the texts at different times, the genres of biblical literature, the problems of critical literary analysis, and the functions of literature as a mode of human discourse and expression. It is certainly hard to conceive of any good biblical course not focusing on these matters with rigorous attention to both detail and substance. For those who go on to further study in the area, exposure to these issues is essential. And even for those who do not expect to study these matters further, the serious study of these historical and literary materials, as well as the methods appropriate to them, can be important elements in a liberal education.

And yet for all their importance, and in spite of their traditional role in introductory courses, standard historical and literary approaches to the Bible have been superseded by a new interdisciplinary phenomenon in biblical studies. In the current educational climate, what goes on in history, literature, philosophy, sociology, anthropology, and other departments in terms of method, and sometimes also content, can be closely related to the work of biblical study. Or to put it the other way around, it is now increasingly the case that the work of serious biblical study requires that one find out what historians, philosophers, sociologists, anthropologists, archaeologists, literary theorists, and so on are thinking about.

Of course in a certain sense biblical studies courses have always been interdisciplinary, as I indicated above when I listed some of the various forms that such courses have taken. However, the interdisciplinary character of biblical studies in the new academic climate is a wholly new phenomenon. One might say that the current interdisciplinary approach is in the process of being created as scholars burst the bounds of traditional biblical study from the inside out. Now it is no longer a matter of simply trying to relate two things to each other across a disciplinary divide—such as history and literature or history and archaeology—but a matter of forging disciplinary links that dissolve the divide and transform the character of the whole enterprise. Now if people across traditional lines of study want to understand the substance of their own respective subjects, they must, as a matter of necessity, talk to each other. Such conversations create new connections and contribute to human understanding. These kinds of encounters also make the intellectual fault lines of our time clearer, and understanding these fault lines is certainly important for anyone wishing to understand our culture.

To the extent that introductory courses on the Bible successfully expose students to this new interdisciplinary character of biblical studies (and, by extension, of the whole academic enterprise), they will foster intellectual integration rather than fragmentation; they can lead people to see the interconnectedness of human life—not the disconnectedness of it. In short, such courses can contribute to the humanizing work of education. For this reason alone, introductory courses in biblical studies should be a central aspect of higher education. And yet when I teach introductory courses on the Bible, my own goals are even more ambitious.

Teaching Goals

When I teach an introductory course on the Bible, I seek to help students learn not only about their world both past and present but also about their own place in that world. It short, it is my intent that the study of the Bible contribute to the examined life for those who have personal religious interests, as well as for those who do not. I do not exclude religious faith and practice from the conversation but instead examine these things in the same way that I examine other aspects of the material. My goal is to create a culture in the classroom that generates critical conversations about all aspects of the material. When I am successful, the learning process is multilateral. Of course, this success is never due simply to my own good intentions and efforts. The students have to help create an atmosphere in the classroom that is conducive to such critical conversations; they have to be active learners and, where possible, teachers in their own right.

One of the reasons I do not exclude religious faith and practice from the conversation is that many students come to the academic study of the Bible and religion for reasons of personal conviction and commitment. Many students come to these classes searching for something of existential significance; they hope to take away something that will be of more than intellectual and educational importance. These are certainly legitimate interests and hopes, and they should not be stifled by an overly narrow view of what is and is not of appropriate academic concern. Within the parameters of academic discourse, these people have a right to shape the educational experience to their own needs and aspirations.

As one who stands within a specific religious tradition myself, I think it is of great significance to learn how to take a serious intellectual approach to the materials of one's religious tradition and still be a practicing member of that tradition. To be sure, clear distinctions must be made between thinking about religion and doing religion; they are different orders of human life. But in the structure of a single human life they are not incompatible, and they should not be so treated. Although the struggle to hold these two things together can be trying and unsettling, it is certainly a worthy goal for many. I, for one, am committed without reservation to the idea that a religious community is enhanced by having the most thoughtful and learned people possible in its ranks. For many people, formal academic study is the route to that end.

In addition to my attempt to create a conversation in the classroom that is open to all and that, in particular, does not exclude matters of religious faith and practice, I insist in all of the biblical studies course I teach that at some point during the semester students struggle with seven specific "problems" in the study of the Bible and religion. These problems do not concern typical matters of biblical content and method; rather, they have to with the full scope of a serious liberal education.

First, I insist that students see that biblical texts and religious phenomena are subject to rational and cogent explanation at many points. In part, this insistence is my way of helping students develop critical thinking skills, but my intention is also to help them overcome the all too convenient assumption that religion is a matter of belief and that belief is not subject to human explanation—or the more extreme variation of this assumption, namely, that religion is simply irrational nonsense. The assumption that religion is beyond explanation because it is a matter of belief is often used as a defensive ploy to protect one's convictions from challenge and critique, whereas the assumption that religion is nonsense is baldly dismissive. Both assumptions display a shallow ignorance that should not, in my judgment, be allowed to stand, if students harbor any claim to being educated in these matters.

Second, I work hard at enabling my students to understand the complex relationships between "material" and "method," between *what* one sees and *how* one came to see that and not something else. Comprehending this relationship between material and method not only helps students understand their own interpretations of the material but also helps them make sense of the work of modern interpreters of biblical texts. Knowing how these interpreters arrived at their conclusions is critical to understanding those conclusions. A knowledge of the structural interactions between "material" and "method" also helps students understand other fields of investigation, such as the social sciences and perhaps even the physical sciences.

Third, I emphasize that my conclusions about biblical texts, as well as students' own conclusions, are not the final word on the subject. These conclusions are installments in an ongoing conversation. Keeping the conversation going may be as important as the specific assertions one wishes to make about the material under consideration. In other words, neither my conclusions nor those of the students are beyond retort. Without critique and counter-critique, the educational process can devolve into silence, where the authority of the teacher wins, and active engagement on the part of all is lost. In these circumstances, learning becomes simply a matter of learning the right answers. Losing a sense of the open-endedness of the conversation can destroy interest in the study of religion about as quickly as anything. Keeping the conversation going can indeed be a struggle for all concerned, but it is a worthy struggle to be sure.

Fourth, I desire that students in my classes achieve a level of intellectual skepticism that provokes their curiosity and drives their imagination. Not only is skepticism necessary in the face of the "lie," but it is crucial in the search for self-understanding. True self-knowledge is hard won and not the result of merely accepting an idea because someone else says so. In the search for self-knowledge, there is a necessary moment of skepticism that compels us to look behind and beyond the immediate, that drives our quest for knowledge and understanding. It prods and goads us into thinking seriously about matters of religion and belief. I also think that a healthy skepticism has the capacity to prevent us from slipping into self-consuming forms of cynicism that undermine intellectual life and erode social engagement. Skepticism in the service of intellectual critique can be compelling, whereas negativism driven to the point of cynicism can be debilitating.

Fifth, I attempt to get my students to see that religion and the Bible are public matters open to observation and analysis. Religion may be a personal matter for many people, but it is not private in the sense that it is beyond discussion or analysis. Likewise, individual biblical interpretations are not beyond critique; they are open to scrutiny and judgment according to modes of analysis appropriate to the context in which they are made. In the context of higher education, these modes include academic rules of discourse, analysis, and rebuttal. If religion and the Bible are not considered public matters, then people can retreat into their own internal realms of belief and prejudice, where personal and intellectual growth are virtually impossible. Moreover, apart from public scrutiny, religious ideas and biblical interpretations, no matter how heartfelt, cease to be subject to moral correction, even when they flirt with sinister ideologies such as anti-Semitism. For these reasons, religion must be treated as the public matter, which in fact it is.

Sixth, I try to impress upon my students how important it is to see that the religions found within the Bible and the religions that have grown out of the Bible are not simply organized around ways of "believing." These religious traditions also involve ways of "behaving," ways of "doing," and, furthermore, they are inherently social. Perhaps because of the influence of the classical Protestant emphasis upon individual faith, many modern Europeans and North Americans define religion as a matter of individual belief—and that it surely is. But religion is also a matter of social practice. To use Jacob Neusner's well-known categories: A religion is a system that involves an "ethnos" (a social group), an "ethos" (a world view), and an "ethic" (a way of life). To understand religion in general and biblical religions in particular, students must study these conceptual issues. In this way, students can begin to see that a religion pervades virtually all aspects of human life. It is not limited to some narrowly circumscribed realm called "religious" life.

Finally, I insist that my students understand the extent to which religion and the Bible have contributed to the general formation of civilization and culture. The Bible and the various religious traditions that stem from it have been powerful contributors to many aspects of numerous cultures we know today. The images and symbols of biblical stories, invigorated by religious passions, have spawned great music, art, architecture, literature, and ideas. For those of us who live in societies that have been formed by these great intellectual and artistic traditions, it is virtually impossible to understand ourselves and our world without understanding that these traditions have biblical and religious roots. Indeed, it is these roots that have shaped who we are, how we think, how we behave, how we organize ourselves as people, as well as the values we hold or reject. Hence, the study of religion and the Bible ought to be an important component of a good liberal education.

Index of Terms
and Names

Index of
Biblical References